TORCH OF FREEDOM

AND THE UNDERGROUND HISTORICAL LEADERS WHO PASSED IT FORWARD

OBSTACLÉS
PRESS

GEORGE GUZZARDO

First Edition, October 2016
10 9 8 7 6 5 4 3 2

Published by:

Obstaclés Press
200 Commonwealth Court
Cary, NC 27511

lifeleadership.com

ISBN 978-0-9976311-8-0

Cover design and layout by Norm Williams, nwa-inc.com

Printed in the United States of America

TORCH OF FREEDOM

CONTENTS

PART I
THE FOUNDATIONS OF FREEDOM: FROM ANCIENT SUMERIA TO GREECE AND ROME

PART II
THE RISE OF CHRISTIANITY

PART III
THE RENAISSANCE AND REFORMATION

PART IV
THE ENLIGHTENMENT

PART V
THE AGE OF REVOLUTION

PART VI
THE AGE OF WORLD WARS AND MODERN TIMES

FOREWORD

In every human society, there are two equal and opposite powers battling for supremacy, a supremacy that neither side can hold indefinitely, swinging back and forth like the arm of a pendulum. The two powers—force and freedom—have been in mortal conflict since time immemorial. The conflict is renewed in every generation to define how society will survive. In the book you hold in your hands, author George Guzzardo shares the story of the freedom fighters, the brave men and women who passed the torch of freedom to the next generation.

The stories presented bring you to the front lines of the conflict, to experience the trials and tribulations as if you were actually there. Perhaps the best compliment an author can receive about one of his books is that it changed the reader. For the best books are not only filled with how-to information, but also why-to inspiration. This is exactly what Guzzardo accomplishes in this work, not only sharing the historical ebb and flow of the freedom tide, but also highlighting the courageous stands, the personal sacrifices, and even the underlying motives that drove those who carried the torch of freedom. Reading their stories will inspire you to play your part in the unfolding drama between force and freedom.

Naturally, the power elites, those who carry the torch of force, seek to coerce and confuse the masses, dividing them through fear and hate, to gain at the masses' expense. By contrast, influential leaders, those who carry the torch of freedom, seek to serve and educate the masses, inspiring in them encouragement and love, to bless everyone within society. Society is blessed or cursed based upon whether freedom or force is in the driver's seat. Hence, the importance of freedom fighters cannot be exaggerated.

Indeed, if we look beneath the surface of freedom-based leadership, we can discern one fundamental fact of influence; namely, from those to whom much is given, much is required. This is what the freedom torch carriers understood, for leadership is only leadership in a culture of freedom, not force. In fact, all the alleged power of leaders is merely the display of confidence the community has in their ability to take them where they want to go. Therefore, any attempt to physically control the community, whatever else it may be called, should certainly not be labeled leadership. Influence is something a leader earns by virtue of character and competence, whereas coercion is the non-leader's substitute for the lack of those qualities.

Moreover, it follows that as coercion increases, true leadership decreases. After all, if the alleged leader actually had the community's buy-in, then why would force need to be applied at all? Unfortunately, societies and communities across the globe have become so inured to the use of force by positional leadership that the difference between influence and intimidation has been blurred beyond recognition. Bureaucratic exercise of force has been applied so steadily that most people are unaware of any other approach to achieving a community's goals.

Nonetheless, there is a better way. In fact, it's the only way that deserves the noble title of leadership. While neglected and abused by its ersatz replacements, true leadership is the art and science of influence without coercion—in short, servant leadership. During the Industrial Revolution, however, servant leadership was replaced with the command-and-control structures modeled upon national militaries. Indeed, Big Government, Big Banks, and Big Corporations (aka Big Bureaucracies) have all defaulted to coercion, rather than service, as the ruling modus operandi. Students of politics, naturally, recognize this trend for what it is—namely, a continuation of what James Madison called "the old trick of turning every contingency into a resource for accumulating force in the government." At the risk of understatement, this has a considerable effect upon how force (coercion) and freedom (service) are balanced in leadership.

For this and many other reasons, I enjoyed Guzzardo's new book, *The Torch of Freedom*. It captures the ongoing story of force and freedom in a succinct yet thorough fashion. The force tide must be checked before the freedom tide will return, and this book will help identify the modern men and women who will stand up and claim their birthright. Freedom isn't free, but I believe life is hardly worth living without it. To put it bluntly, I simply do not believe our forebears intended to sacrifice so much for freedom so that we could whimper in servitude. The thought is ludicrous!

Then what are we waiting for? Let's dive into *The Torch of Freedom*, accept the torch from our ancestors, and pass it to our descendants. After all, from those to whom much is given, much is required.

Sincerely,

Orrin Woodward,

New York Times Best-Selling Author and

Inc Magazine Top 20 Leader

PREFACE

In my research and development of this book, I wrote several blogs. One in particular, "Historical Leaders who Passed the Torch of Freedom", I asked for feedback from those who follow my blog and here I share some of the comments received:

Randy Crain said...

"One of my favorite stories to hear about is George Washington Carver. Born in 1864 he used what he had, spent his days exploring, and was described as "having a burning zeal to know everything." He was deeply practical and turned simple things into major products and ideas. Using peanuts, created hundreds of ideas, products, and became a legend. He found happiness and honor in helping the world. He became a role model to the African-American community."

Jeremy Pethke said...

"Thank you, George, for your continued study into the meanings behind freedom and liberty. Before diving into Life Leadership's information, I didn't care about freedom or what it stood for. I just thought I would follow in my parent's footsteps and just live an average life. I believe we are in the midst of history's greatest shift in influential leaders that the world has ever known. But for that shift to happen there had to have been a long list of leaders who passed the torch. One of those leaders of old that passed that torch was Sir Winston Churchill.

When the call for leadership arose, Churchill stepped up and grabbed the torch of freedom. He didn't stand by as his country was overtaken. He did his duty. I believe there has never been a greater call for duty and honor than today. We are at a turning point and we have two choices, 1. Stand by and let the torch of freedom burn out for our children and grandchildren, or 2. Stand up and grab the torch of freedom and reinstate our liberties and light the torch so bright and hot that it will never be put out again. It will take courage, but more importantly, it will take action! Who will stand up? If not us, then who?"

Steve Del Castillo said...

"One of my favorite heroes, as regarding the passing of the torch of freedom, is Sir Winston Churchill. Churchill united a nation, led a people, and eventually inspired the free world to rise up against the tyranny of Hitler and his Nazi evil in World War 2. I believe that he was a voice in the wilderness, shouting out in spite of popular voice until proven right. And then, when the rest of Britain accepted the truth of what was happening, he managed to lead them through some of the most dismal and dark years in history, in a fight that seemed impossible and for a cause almost lost. The torch was flickering low in those dark days."

I named my son after Sir Winston, in tribute to his foresight and leadership. On a different, but not unrelated note, I am proud to be in battle with you sir. Our cause too seems daunting, but is as important as was Winston's for the passing of the torch.

Dwayne & Jill Walkowski said...

"George, there were many important figures in our history that carried the torch of freedom and we should be grateful for them. Personally, this makes me think of a man in my local community who I am grateful for, who carried and still carries the torch of freedom. Harvey Hyslop fought in the Korean War and has received two bronze stars. He came in as an enlisted man and left as an officer. Out of the 406 men in his platoon, only 16 of them made it out alive.

His story deeply scarred him, and after many years of silence, he has found the courage to share what happened during that time. He speaks at the local high school now to tell his story. He is a strong Christian man who attends church every week, walks the walk, and mentors with the younger generations. He is also actively involved in our community, speaks up with various articles in the newspaper, and takes a stand politically. In addition to the many other important figures in history, it is men like Harvey, who have carried the torch of freedom for decades without glamour in our local communities, who have my admiration. He is finishing strong."

Shanna Krueger said...

"There are so many leaders already mentioned that are exceptional, including the leaders of Life Leadership, and you and the other founders' undying passion to lead us all to freedom and greatness. Thank you.

I can't help but mention Victor Frankyl as I finish his book, "A Man's Search for Meaning". His belief and thinking, and the meaning he gave to all the horrific acts going on...he helped himself endure and his belief that freedom would come helped so many because they borrowed his belief. He didn't stop there, but continued to help others seek out their meaning in their lives in the worst of times. Living through Auschwitz would have done long-term harm to anyone emotionally, yet this man took a different angle and took the lead to understand there was purpose in his suffering. Truly inspiring."

Steve Duba said...

Thank you, George, for your diligence. We are in need of more inspirational leaders like you to continue moving the torch forward. Recently I dug in to the history of a man named William Bradford. Wow. Perseverance would be to light a word. (1590-1657). He was an English Separatist (Pilgrim). Numerous deaths in his early years throughout his family. He was an orphan at age 7 and lost his wife on the Mayflower. He refused to live under the tyranny of King James. That brought him to Plymouth and the early settlement of our nation. So much history in his personal story about following. His most famous work was the history of the founding of the Plymouth Colony. A true carrier of the freedom torch.

Bud Carton said...

"I am a Veteran of the Vietnam Era, and have found George Guzzardo to be a fabulous educator and inspirational speaker. Mr Guzzardo explains not only our American history and why it is important, but how the world events had played such an important role in our country's inception. Tyranny, and many different forms of oppression, ignites our human souls for self governing and prosperity. People should be inspired to fight for a cause and put God's armor on for safety and strength.

People with honor and integrity need to stand tall and keep our country's history alive, while everyone is trying to modernize our world to make it comfortable. Taking action, being accountable and preserving why our country became great, is our duty for our preservation. Our Forefathers drafted documents to have our country lead in a respectable fashion. The government that is elected by the people is to represent and preserve their voices. Government was not created to dictate or run the people's to serve their objectives. We the people should be inspired by the meaning and direction that George Guzzardo is taking us...back to our future."

Brian Bailey said...

"I'm thoroughly impressed with the responses, and the wealth of historical leadership examples listed. I'm excited to see many of these comments in your new book. I concur with many of the historical leaders listed. I would have to add the Apostle Paul (I don't believe I saw him listed). Just diving in to the Epistles in the New Testament, we see Paul preaching many concepts of freedom, ultimately rooted in the Gospel, which is the premise for all freedom in spiritual freedom. When you understand whose you are, oppression can't prevail."

Phillip said...

"Great blog George! I would say William Wilberforce, from what I've read about him he was a young man searching for a cause, then God laid something in his lap, slave trade, he did not expect nor knew if he should accept. His heart could not deny what he needed to do so he picked up the torch, despite the amount of "wind" he had to fight to keep it alive, not only from adversaries but also from loved ones! His unrelenting persistence to stay the course all those years even through his own personal sickness was absolutely inspiring!

All of the examples here that are mentioned should be the ones in the textbooks kids are learning about! It is definitely imperative we bring to light examples like these to everyone we meet so the torch from our generation, that is at a dimming flicker, stands a fighting chance for the next generations to come."

Ben Alexander said...

"Another leader whose teachings led to an increase in freedom was the 18th century Scottish philosopher Adam Smith, specifically his magnum opus; The Wealth of Nations.

While a bit controversial at the time, Adam Smith laid the intellectual foundation for the formation of free market economics.

It is capitalism and free market economics that has created the modern global middle class, a group that has more freedom and a higher standard of living than any previous group in human history. Free enterprise gives rise to more economic options, and the success of the United States and the freedoms we enjoy are partially due to the continued prosperity of our Republic.

As an American and the owner of 2 profitable businesses I get to enjoy the realization of free market economics 226 years after the death of Adam Smith. The United States represents only 5% of the world population yet generates 22% of the annual global wealth (as measured in GDP) mainly because we have taken Adam Smith's concepts and combined them with English Common Law to create the system we enjoy today."

Scott Hosie said...

"Frederic Bastiat was a political thought leader in his time that not only passed on the Torch of Freedom, but has influenced others to do the same. What he wrote still has influence today. Bastiat's ideas and writings have positively influenced our economic & political freedoms, and stand directly in the face of socialism and communism. In "The Law" he writes:

"All people have had laws. But few people have been happy. Why is this so? Because the legislators themselves have almost always been ignorant of the purpose of society, which is the uniting of families by a common interest."

This incredibly simple and accurate statement shows the firm grasp Bastiat had on freedom and human society."

Barry Quinn said...

"A leader I think of is Grand Master Jean de la Valette, of the Knights of St. John of Malta. He led 600 Knights and 6000 soldiers against an invading Turkish army of 30,000 soldiers to defend Christianity. Without their bravery and relentless fighting, Christianity may have been lost to all of Europe. They definitely passed the Torch of Freedom."

John Feldhouse said...

"Perhaps in a more modern era, Bob Kahn and Vint Cerf who are often attributed to helping produce the modern internet. With all the things bad and good that have come from the internet, its force is almost, if not greater, than the printing press. I bet you ask though, "Why would you consider Bob and Vint passers of the freedom torch?"

I think the internet has opened up so many new avenues in which freedom is able to be earned. I look at Egypt as one primary example and how they were able to use the internet to gain leverage. Of course, this freedom is not as obvious as past times, but I do feel it's a strong force for the future of freedom."

Michael Robinson said...

"I actually have the Leader that really carried the Torch of Freedom. a man called LIEUTENANT GENERAL LEWIS "CHESTY" B. PULLER, USMC. Lieutenant General Lewis "Chesty" Burwell Puller, colorful veteran of the Korean fighting, four World War II campaigns and expeditionary service in China, Nicaragua and Haiti, was one of the most decorated Marines in the Corps, and the only Leatherneck ever to win the Navy Cross five times for heroism and gallantry in action.

Promoted to his final rank and placed on the temporary disability retired list 1 November 1955, he died on 11 October 1971 in Hampton, Virginia after a long illness. By his unflagging determination, he served to inspire his men to heroic efforts in defense of their positions and assured the safety of much valuable equipment which would otherwise have been lost to the enemy. His skilled leadership, superb courage and valiant devotion to duty in the face of overwhelming odds reflect the highest credit upon Colonel Puller and the United States Naval Service.

This Marine carried the Torch of Freedom."

Lena said...

"What a great story. A leader that came to mind was Harriet Tubman. I've always been inspired by how she rescued slaves, even when her health was very poor. She had a big impact on many slaves. When I was a child I was always fascinated by people with so much courage. Like you George, I often read classical literature and didn't even know what a difference it could make in a person's life. That's who came to mind."

Randy Wooten said...

"A couple come to my mind - I think what is most powerful for me are their examples.

Cincinnatus in Rome in 458 B.C. He had once held the highest office in the land but, through events, had lost that wealth and was happy being a farmer, tilling the land. When the Aequi attacked the Roman army, the leaders went to Cincinnatus because he was wise and respected to ask his help. They told him how the Roman army had been trapped and asked him to head an army to rescue them. They gave him power to do whatever he wanted. So he took some boys and the guards of the city, armed them, and went.

He was victorious in relieving the trapped Roman army. As a leader, his word had become law. But after doing what he was asked to do he went to the Roman leaders, returned the station they had given him and went back to farming. He had been in power for 16 days. But somehow he didn't let it get to his head. Sometimes we feel like we are too busy to have to deal with freedom stuff. He showed that we can take time out and be that person who can make a difference.

INTRODUCTION

I've always been intrigued by science fiction movies and the idea of time travel. What if time travel really was possible? What if we could travel back to four thousand years ago in seconds? What if we could observe in action some of the greatest leaders in history who have passed the torch of freedom? What wisdom and timeless lessons could we learn?

Physical time travel is not yet a reality. Yet every one of us has the opportunity to travel back in time in the pages of history. Lessons abound, yet few people ever learn them because they fail to study history.

Sometimes the torch of freedom is handed to us unsuspectingly. That's what happened to me about forty years ago while I suffered through public school. From a young age, I felt as if I was being programmed at school—not truly educated. I wanted badly to leave. However, my homeroom teacher made a bargain with me: If I stayed in class, I could sit on the windowsill and read any book of my choosing. Instead of participating in normal classes, I began to read Shakespeare and other great classics. Today I recognize the unexpected benefits from receiving a self-directed classical education.

America's Founders received the torch of freedom in the same way. Two-thirds of the signers of the Declaration of Independence studied the classics, half of them informally. Unfortunately, self-directed classical education has been on a steep decline for decades.

Between 1971 and 1991 the number of classics majors in America dropped by 30 percent. Today, out of a million bachelor's degrees awarded, only 600 are granted in the classics.

Our curriculums used to concentrate on great classical works, such as the writings of Cicero, the poetry of Virgil and Homer, the histories of Xenophon, and the Greek New Testament. This was important because as Professor of History Carl J. Richard said, "Classical ideas provided the basis for the theories of government, social responsibility, human nature, and virtue." In addition, the classics teach the principles of treachery, bondage, and heroism. They share the greatest stories from the greatest leaders—their dreams, struggles, and victories.

Today, instead of learning the timeless values and principles that history provides, our educational system has watered down history to textbook lists of names, dates, and facts, which seem irrelevant to our daily lives. This is having a profound negative effect on freedom. This amnesia about our origin dooms us to repeat the painful lessons of the past.

My interest in writing about this group of historical leaders and the lessons they taught is to ignite your passion and what it means to have the opportunity to share in carrying the torch of freedom. I invite you to walk through time with me as we rediscover those great historical leaders who kept the torch burning bright and carried it to us.

PART I

THE FOUNDATIONS OF FREEDOM: FROM ANCIENT SUMERIA TO GREECE AND ROME

In Mesopotamia we find what is called the cradle of Western civilization. Located in Mesopotamia's southern tip is Sumeria, or modern-day Iraq and Kuwait. It is there in Sumeria where the first civilization came to be. This area had all the essential elements necessary to support widespread development and population growth, including abundant food, year-round water supplies, and building materials.

The freedom to harvest these raw materials was the lighting of the "torch of freedom." By applying our ideas, talents, and energy to create and innovate with the raw materials we have been given, we have the opportunity to reach our full,

God-given potential. This is the ultimate fulfillment in life: inherently, we crave to be everything we were created to be.

As people learned to take advantage of the fertile waters of the Euphrates and Tigris, the Sumerian population exploded—the first fruits of freedom. This expansion resulted in habitation density greater than any that had occurred before anywhere in the world. Hamlets turned to villages and villages to towns, towns became cities, and cities stretched into metropolitan areas. The development and resultant security meant that people could live a more stable life, not solely focused on day-to-day survival and daily combat. Now that people were united into smaller geographic areas and division of labor was increased, not only was food in greater supply, but so was security.

Not everyone, however, found this "civilized" way of life desirable. As we witness around us then and now, there is another side of human nature. The dark side of humanity is rooted in pride and craves power and control. These forces have been and always will be in constant play.

The surrounding desert areas were considerably less fertile, and survival in the deserts required a more austere, nomad-herder lifestyle. This lifestyle also offered more liberty to roam and greater independence. The nomadic way of life, while harsher and less secure, was unencumbered with taxes, laws, or kings.

At the same time the agrarian-based city dwellers were establishing themselves, the desert nomads were also developing their own way of life. The city dwellers viewed the nomads as harsh and uncouth. The nomads viewed the city dwellers as soft and weak. Over time inevitable clashes resulted. At first only Sumeria's borders were at risk of attack, but early on the first pattern of war was established and then repeated over and over again.

Out in the desert a powerful nomad leader would arise. The nomad would conquer or recruit neighboring nomad tribes to join him in arms. Their combined forces, though outnumbered, were expert in weaponry and warfare. The unarmed, "soft" agrarian townsfolk had little chance against the cruel desert forces.

This is where we first observe what best-selling author Orrin Woodward calls "the Physical Matrix," one of the three forms of control in the matrix: human slavery. The conquering nomads handily subjected the farmers to slavery, while positioning themselves as the non-laboring ruling class of kings, princes, oligarchs, and the like. Taxes, laws, and corruption, favoring those in power, began to multiply, and the torch of freedom was reduced to a flicker. Liberty was extinguished.

Generations passed. As we will witness throughout time, people who oppress are always doomed from the minute they begin to oppress; oppression carries within it the seeds of its own destruction. The hardiness and tenacity that won the conquerors their position disappeared as they grew to enjoy the easy, luxurious life and began to emulate those whom they once conquered. They became complacent, ignoring the cries of the oppressed. The next round of invaders would sweep in, sometimes supported by the oppressed laboring class, and always ripe with hunger, hardened by the harsh realities of life on the edge, and anxious to establish their place in the order.

Century followed century, tyrant followed tyrant, and the passage of a thousand years finally, out of necessity, brought forth a new form of government: democracy. With the birth of Greece around 800 BC, democratic government emerged for the first time. Slavery still existed, but among the citizens a new power arose: the ability to represent themselves in government.

Solon, or "the great lawgiver" as he came to be known, established methods for poor citizens to become members of the legislative assembly and vote. Cleisthenes later expanded democracy by giving every voting member equal rights and making legislative membership dependent on a random drawing.

Never before had the common people had a say in government. Never before had freedom been so close to the everyday citizen and, in fact, relied on everyone's participation in government. True democracy is where citizens participate in government to ensure that their God-given liberties are preserved. We find early in civilization the need to encourage the study and understanding of politics, which is a good thing for liberty and the torch of freedom. But challenges arose in that it was also cumbersome, costly, and unmanageable across wide geographic areas.

Rome partially solved this problem. She furthered the development of free government when her people, in 509 BC, overthrew their conquering neighbors. Rather than crowning a king, they established a representative government where all adult male descendants of the founders were considered citizens and could participate in government. Republicanism was less demanding, less costly, and more manageable across vast areas and disparate peoples.

These developments in government may seem small and insignificant, but it is these examples from history that the American Founders studied and knew by heart, through self-directed education. The roots of liberty, they understood, were found in the fertile soils of Sumeria, Greece, and Rome. The study of these early civilizations still has much to teach us today about freedom and oppression and about monarchy, democracy, and republicanism.

However, without a working knowledge of the principles of freedom, history repeats itself. If vigilance is not maintained and the torch of freedom is left unattended, it is left vulnerable to be extinguished by those who crave power at the expense of liberty.

CHAPTER 1

THE CLAY CONES
OF FREEDOM

S am's work was to reveal secrets that other experts had been
struggling with for decades. It was ironic, since it took decades
for Sam's own calling to be revealed.

He was born to Jewish parents in 1897 in the Russian Empire
under the reign of Czar Nicholas II. Forced to flee Russia because
of the czar's anti-Semitic pogroms, his family ended up in
Philadelphia, where his father established a Hebrew school.

After graduating from South Philadelphia High School, Sam
toyed with a variety of occupations, trying to find his niche. He
taught at his father's school, became a writer, and tried his hand at
business.

Nothing seemed to fit. As he approached the age of thirty, he
had no career and no clear direction. "Finally," he said, "it came to
me that I might well go back to my beginnings and try to utilize
the Hebrew learning on which I had spent so much of my youth,
and relate it in some way to an academic future."

He enrolled at Dropsie College of Philadelphia for Hebrew and
Cognate Learning and became fascinated with Egyptology. He then

transferred to the Oriental Studies Department of the University of Pennsylvania, working with the "brilliant young Ephraim Avigdor Speiser, who was to become one of the world's leading figures in Near Eastern Studies." Speiser was trying to decipher cuneiform tablets of the Late Bronze Age dating from about 1300 BC.

Sam had found his lifelong work: to understand the ancient Sumerian cuneiform writing system. After earning his PhD in 1929, he became famous for his role in the "recovery, restoration, and resurrection of Sumerian literature." He brought together cuneiform tablets that had become distributed among different institutions around the world and spent decades poring over them, trying to decipher their meaning.

In his work he found clay cones dating back to 2300 BC from the Sumerian city-state of Lagash.

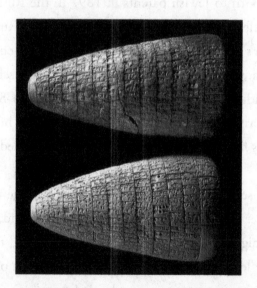

On these cones, which became known as the "Liberty Cones," Sam discovered the world's first documented legal reforms, the first bill of rights, and the first written appearance of the word *freedom*.

Below is a copy of the text on one of the cones. At bottom left, the Sumerian word for freedom, the "amar-gi" symbol, is circled.

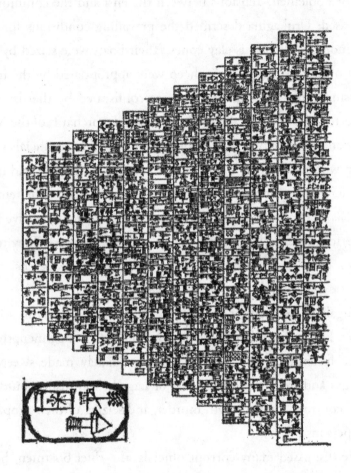

The cones detailed the legal reforms of a king named Urukagina, who reigned over the city of Lagash for seven years, around 2375 BC. Urukagina came into power at a time when Lagash's power and prestige were on the decline. From what little is known of him, he was not of royal descent and was a commoner, which perhaps explains his populist reforms.

Urukagina's immediate predecessor, Lugalanda, had a reputation for greed and corruption. He created an aristocracy with the *ensi* or noblemen. Tensions between the ensi and the community increased. Urukagina described the prevailing conditions for the common people on his clay cones. Their boats were seized by the chief of the boatmen. Their sheep were appropriated by the head herdsman, and their fish stores were confiscated by the fisheries inspector. The "men of the ensi" cut down the orchards of the poor and conscripted workers to labor in the fields. Court officials were "everywhere." The ensi took the best land for themselves and used the sacred oxen from the temples to plow their fields. The temple officials were also greedy and corrupt. They charged excessive fees to perform their religious rituals and to bury the dead. They took bribes, levied onerous taxes which they shared with the ensi, and likewise used temple oxen to plow their fields.

Lugalanda reigned for less than six years before Urukagina seized power. He declared that he was acting on behalf of boatmen, shepherds, fishermen, and farmers. He immediately made sweeping changes and freed the inhabitants of Lagash from usury, burdensome controls, hunger, theft, murder, and seizure of their property and persons.

He dismissed many corrupt officials, the chief boatmen, head herdsmen, and fishery inspectors who had seized private property. He confiscated the estates of the ensi and placed them under the jurisdiction of the gods (i.e., the temples). He removed many court officials, including the supervisors who controlled the grain tax. He dismissed the priests who had taken bribes and the temple administrators who had shared tax revenues with the ensi. He then set limits on the amount that the priests could collect for their religious rituals and their fees for burying the dead.

One of Urukagina's most radical reforms was to cancel debt-slavery and declare a general amnesty for the citizens of Lagash, even for criminals, including thieves and murderers (the clay cones state, "Their prison he cleared out"). It was here that we find this most precious relic: the earliest recorded use of the word *freedom*. The literal translation of the symbol means "return to the mother." Early monarchs used indebtedness for taxes as a means of binding the people for service to the king. To release one back to one's family was often literally to be returned to one's mother. Urukagina's reform to release large segments of the population from such compulsory service was called "amar-gi," meaning they were at liberty to return home.

Urukagina also provided charity for the poor and the elderly. All the reforms were recorded on Urukagina's cones so that "the orphan or widow to the powerful will not be subjugated."

The "Liberty Cones" of Urukagina, as translated by Assyriologist Samuel Noah Kramer, are the world's first documented effort to establish the basic legal rights of citizens. Nothing else like them can be found in ancient history. Although very few people know about them, they are just as important as the Magna Carta or the American Bill of Rights.

Sam Kramer died at age 93 in 1990. Thanks to his tireless work, the world knows of the first bill of rights—not the one enshrined in the first ten amendments of the US Constitution but the one preserved on four-thousand-year-old clay cones and created by a freedom fighter named Urukagina. This is where the torch of freedom was ignited.

LESSONS FROM URUKAGINA ON HOW TO PASS THE TORCH

1. Freedom fighters break the bonds of oppression. They are not in it for themselves. They fight not for personal privilege but rather for the rights of everyone—and especially commoners. They seek not to expand their own power but to improve the lives of others.

2. Tyranny ensues when one group of people is given special favors over other groups. Establishing a level playing field stops manipulation.

3. Freedom is protected and expanded when it is codified into a legal code and everyone is treated equally before the law. Through literacy come knowledge and awareness.

CHAPTER 2

A LONE WOLF RETURNS HOME TO SERVE HIS PEOPLE

I was born the son of a king and given a name meaning "Deed of a Wolf." I suppose it was fitting, given that much of my life was spent as a lone wolf far from home.

I was born at a time when our kingdom was plagued by lawlessness and civil strife. My own father was stabbed and killed with a butcher knife as he was attempting to quell a riot. The kingship passed to my brother. I was next in line, should anything happen to my brother.

Indeed, my brother did not rule long before he died, leaving me as king and his wife with child. When my sister-in-law gave birth to my nephew, I named him "Joy of the People" and gave him the right to the crown, as he was the son of the king. I held the kingship as a stewardship, waiting for my nephew to come of age.

Despite my best intentions, my sister-in-law, the mother of my nephew, and her relatives envied and hated me. She spread rumors about me, even saying that I was plotting the death of her son. This weighed heavily on me. Given that times were dangerous, I knew it was all too possible that he could be killed—and that I would be blamed for it.

I decided that the best thing for my kingdom would be to relinquish the throne and leave until my nephew had grown and fathered a son to secure the succession. I gave up all authority and traveled to a nearby island. I spent a long time there, studying their civilization and government, taking careful notes of things that could be useful for my homeland.

After learning what I needed to learn, I traveled to another country, which was much different than my own. I compared their love of pleasure to the soberness of my countrymen and thought of how the two could be combined. While there, I also discovered the works of a great poet who had written two epic poems rich in lessons on statecraft and morality. I studied his works diligently and determined to make his works widely known.

I continued my travels, this time turning south to an exotic land in the desert. My cultural studies continued as well. I was struck by how this people separated their military from menial workers. My homeland, I decided, would be well served to have a professional military as well.

It was then that I received a letter from my countrymen, begging me to come back. They told me that I was the king in their hearts. Even the kings asked me to return because they believed I could protect them from the people. I had studied and learned much. I was not eager for power, but I believed I could apply the lessons I had learned from other civilizations to create a new era for my country. I decided to return home.

When I returned, the first thing I did was consult the priestess of our temple and ask her for guidance. She told me that my prayers had been heard and that the state that observed my laws would become the most famous in the world. With her bold endorsement, I went to the leading men of my country and enlisted their support. When I had gained enough support, the crown fell upon me, and I was free to institute my reforms.

The first thing I did was create a council of elders, of whom twenty-eight had to be over the age of sixty. The remaining two were the ruling kings, regardless of their age. I decreed that the twenty-eight council members other than the kings would be elected and would serve for life. The council debated motions which were to be put before the citizen assembly and also functioned as a court with the authority to try any Spartan, including kings. One historian at the time explained that the council "allays and qualifies the fiery genius of the royal office" and gives stability and safety to the commonwealth, like the ballast in a ship.

You must understand how revolutionary this was: Prior to this, our government had always been an absolute monarchy. This was the first time the people's voice was heard. Previously, my country had swung back and forth between the extremes of democracy and tyranny: anarchy and dictatorship. The elected council I created resisted those extremes. Another effect was that I secured complete and undivided allegiance from the citizens.

That was just the beginning of my reforms. One of the greatest challenges my country faced was extreme inequality. Wealth was concentrated in the hands of very few people. I equalized landholdings and wealth among the population. My biographer explained, "To the end, therefore, that he might expel from the state arrogance and envy, luxury and crime, and those yet more inveterate diseases of want and superfluity, he obtained of them to renounce their properties, and to consent to a new division of the land, and that they should all live together on an equal footing; merit to be their only road to eminence...."

Applying lessons I had learned in my travels, I also created a professional military. When healthy boys turned seven years old, they were placed in a rigorous military regiment aimed at developing leadership, courage, public spirit, and wisdom. Thus, our citizens became strong, and we established a foundation that would serve us well for many generations.

After my reforms I became known for three things: equality, military fitness, and self-discipline. After establishing a new constitution and society, I made my citizens take an oath that they would keep my laws and then, returning to my lone wolf ways, I walked away and disappeared.

As fate would have it, however, I did not disappear from history. You know me as Lycurgus, the lawgiver of Sparta. My legend has continued throughout the ages, and you can find my image on the south wall of the US Supreme Court building in Washington DC.

LESSONS FROM LYCURGUS ON HOW TO PASS THE TORCH

1. Be a lifelong student of history, society, government, and freedom. Observe nations and see what works and what doesn't work. Don't just spout unfounded opinions—be learned enough to have an intelligent perspective.

2. Monarchies, aristocracies, and democracies simply do not work. Free government is mixed government, which integrates elements of all forms of government to create separation of powers and checks and balances.

3. Never be a zealot for power. Be willing to walk away from prestigious positions when it is the right thing and creates better circumstances for other people.

CHAPTER 3

BIG HEAD, SMALL EGO

H ad he lived in our age, young students might call him an "egghead." That probably would be kinder than what his peers in his age called him.

He was born in 495 BC to a noble and politically active family in Athens. His parents named him Pericles, meaning "Surrounded by Glory." The name turned out to be highly appropriate, as he would be surrounded by glory throughout his life and cloaked in glory in the pages of history. And it was certainly a better name than his nickname.

As a child and young man he was quiet and introverted. He avoided public appearances, preferring instead to devote his time to his studies. Thanks to his family's nobility and wealth, he was able to get the best education Athens offered. He learned music from the masters of the time and enjoyed the company of the most highly regarded philosophers, Protagoras, Zeno of Elea, and Anaxagoras. Through his education and the influence of his friends, he cultivated a calm and self-control that became proverbial.

In short, he was a pensive and thoughtful bookworm. That, combined with the fact that he had an unusually large head, created his nickname: "Squill-head," after the squill, a type of sea onion that grows a large bulb. Thankfully, Pericles learned to master his emotions and let criticism slide off his back, which would serve him well in his career and the establishment of his legacy.

In his early thirties, Pericles began accepting positions of leadership and became active in Athenian politics. Never one for the limelight, he protected his privacy and sought to present himself as a model for his fellow citizens. For example, he would often avoid banquets in order to be frugal.

Pericles became increasingly active and aggressive in his political pursuits. He joined with the democratic party to reduce the power of the traditional council controlled by the Athenian aristocracy. The Athenian Assembly accepted the proposal without opposition, signaling the beginning of a new era of "radical democracy."[1] The democratic party gradually became dominant in Athens.

Pericles promoted a populist social policy. For example, he proposed that the poor be permitted to watch theatrical plays without paying. He granted generous wages on citizens who served as jurymen. He enacted legislation granting the lower classes access to the political system and public offices. His goal was to raise the *demos*, or common people, which he saw as the main source of Athenian power.

In 461 BC, when the leader of the democratic party, Ephialtes, was murdered, Pericles seized the opportunity to consolidate his power. He became the unchallenged leader of the party and, with no opposition, the ruler of Athens. There he would remain until his death in 429, and his rule would later be referred to as the "Age of Pericles," the golden age of Greece.

He set out to secure Athens' cultural and political leadership among the Greek city-states. In 454 BC, he led military excursions against Sparta and her allies during the First Peloponnesian War. He built the largest navy at the time and dominated the Mediterranean Sea. The war eventually ended nine years later with a peace treaty between Athens and Sparta.

Pericles also spearheaded a magnificent building project centered on the Acropolis, a high rocky outcrop above the city of Athens that housed the Parthenon, the Propylaia, the Erechtheion, and the Temple of Athena Nike. The architecture was by far the grandest and most expensive that had been built in Greece up to that point. In addition, Pericles heavily promoted the arts and literature. The era of "Periclean" art and architecture became the wonder of the world.

Under his leadership, democracy in Athens rose to its pinnacle. He was popular and was repeatedly elected to political office by the citizens of Athens. He influenced free speech by his tolerance of literature that was even critical to him. Plutarch described him as "manifestly free from all forms of corruption, and superior to all considerations of money."

It was principally Pericles' influence that gave Athens its reputation of being the educational and cultural center of ancient Greece. Classicist C. E. Robinson wrote, "Athens' heyday lasted less than eighty years, yet, a handful of men attempted more and achieved more in a wider variety of fields than any nation had ever attempted."

Unfortunately, after his death the democratic form of government he had promoted began to degenerate as corruption crept in. As Greek democracy gradually collapsed, it became clear that a mixed form of government would be more effective. Plato's pupil, Aristotle, made a mixed form of government his centerpiece in his book *Politics*. John Adams, an American Founder and ardent proponent of mixed government, learned about the faults of democracy from reading the classics. He wrote, "Simple democracies like Athens were but a transient glare of glory, which passes away like a flash of lightning."

Notwithstanding the flaws of democracy, Pericles left an immortal legacy from which much can be learned. He has been lauded as "the ideal type of the perfect statesman in ancient Greece."[2] Because of his statesmanship, the torch of freedom was advanced for all of humanity. He may have had a big head, but his ego was small, and his heart was pure.

LESSONS FROM PERICLES ON HOW TO PASS THE TORCH

1. Education matters! The foundation of Pericles' statesmanship was the self-directed classical education he received. If we wish to pass the torch of freedom, we must be educated in the classics of history, literature, science, art, and culture.

2. Culture flourishes when people are free. Freedom allows for initiative, and initiative spurs economic, architectural, and artistic advances.

3. Democracy is good to a certain extent. However, in a pure form, it never lasts. Although Pericles had good intentions, a mixed government would have lasted longer.

CHAPTER 4

WHERE CAN YOU BUY VIRTUE?

The handsome young man walked quickly through the narrow lane, head down, lost in thought. He almost tripped on the rod, stretched out purposefully in front of him. It blocked his path, and when it remained in place he looked up in surprise. Who would wish to stop him here?

"Excuse me," the elderly stranger addressed him politely. "Would you kindly tell an inquiring soul, where are the best tunics sold?"

The young man knew just where to direct the man. He promptly replied, indicating where he should look.

"Thank you," the stranger continued. "And if I were in need of sandals, where might I find an excellent pair?"

Again, the young man's reply was quick and astute.

"If I were in need of a good belt, could you direct me where I might find that as well?"

The young man answered each question thoughtfully and intelligently, while the older man continued to inquire after one piece of clothing or another.

"You have been very helpful," the elder concluded. "I have but one more question for you. Where do men become honorable and virtuous?"

The young man paused. The earlier questions had been easy, but this was a question worth deeply pondering. He hesitated and then responded, "I confess, sir, I do not know."

The older man replied, "Follow me, then, and learn."

Thus Socrates began his mentorship of one of the world's great historians, soldiers, and memoirists: Xenophon.

Little is known of Xenophon's early years. His father, Gryllis, had a farm just an hour's horse ride from the great city of Athens. His family, members of the equestrian class, were well enough off that Xenophon was well educated from his youth and received early military training. The Peloponnesian War, a long-drawn-out war between Sparta and Athens, came to a close when he was still just a boy, but the tensions that remained from that war would shape his life in important ways.

Xenophon, philosopher and pragmatist alike, spent much time at Socrates' side and thereby developed his own unique philosophic views and bent. As much as he loved learning, however, he was also a man of action, and when he received a letter from his friend, Proxenus, petitioning him to join him on a military venture and promising an introduction to the great Spartan leader Cyrus, he knew he must join his friend.

Cyrus the Younger, jealous of his older brother's Persian rule and power, had concocted a plan to dethrone his sibling. King Artaxerxes II had a massive army and even greater wealth, and Cyrus knew his troops would be loath to fight so powerful a foe.

Undeterred, Cyrus raised an army, known as "the ten thousand," under the guise of fighting a loathed neighbor, the Pisidians.

Once on their way, however, the army soon realized they were headed not to fight the Pisidians but rather Artaxerxes II. Only with great effort were they convinced to continue on their march. Cyrus led the men valiantly in battle, and his troops were considered to have won, although at great cost. Cyrus was killed in the first conflict, and things quickly went from bad to worse. After the battle the top five generals were invited to a "peace treaty" meeting turned death trap, where all five were executed.

The ten thousand mercenaries were in trouble; they were deep in enemy territory, their leaders were dead, and winter was quickly approaching. They were greatly outnumbered, and it looked like all was lost when a leader to the side of the troops began shouting orders to reorganize the phalanx. With the organization improved, the leader began to communicate tactics and the tide of the fight quickly turned in favor of the Greeks. Afterward, one of the Greek captains asked who had taken charge and won the day. No one seemed to know. Later, it was discovered that it was Xenophon.

During times of trial it's vital to take control of one's destiny, as did Xenophon. The new leader safely led the troops through the conflicts that arose as they slowly made their way back to Athens. Upon their arrival home, he handed the military reins over to the Spartan general Thibron. What should have been a joyous homecoming, however, was bittersweet. Because of his close association with Spartan generals and his participation in fighting Artaxerxes, a proclaimed friend of Athens, he was now exiled from his home country.

Throughout the ensuing years Xenophon wrote a canon of works that have stood the test of time, many of which were the first of their genre—the first biographical novel (*Education of Cyrus*), the first known first-person military memoir (*Anabasis*), and the first continued history (*Hellenica*). From horsemanship to tax law, democracy and oligarchy, Xenophon wrote across a wide range of subjects with clarity and adeptness. His works expose the foibles of monarchy and the weakness of pure democracy and illustrate the value of a mixed government. His histories offer invaluable lessons and observations about early democratic leaders and ideas. His biographies lend perceptive insight into the life of Socrates, Cyrus, and others.

His influence stretches through antiquity, the Middle Ages, and early modernity down to contemporary times. His works are some of the first transcribed by students of ancient Greek, because of their straightforward and succinct wording. Alexander the Great used his works as a field guide for his conquest of Persia, and philosophers ranging from Machiavelli to Shaftesbury and John Adams studied his works as a key part of their classical education.

The "Attic Muse" left the world with a legacy of literature and leadership that freedom fighters today would do well to study and emulate.

LESSONS FROM XENOPHON ON HOW TO PASS THE TORCH

1. Mentors play a crucial role in preparing for leadership. While Xenophon developed his own perspectives on government, Socrates' tutelage helped him learn to question, reason, and inspire others in ways he could not have learned on his own.

2. Great results come from applying what you have learned. Courageous action aligned with competence creates influence and demands respect.

3. Education takes time and effort. Without the learning opportunities and time that wealth provided Xenophon, he might never have been the great philosopher, author and strategist that we know him to be. Today we have easy access to educational tools, but if we don't use them, we're no better able to impact liberty than were the Athenian underclass.

CHAPTER 5

THE UNLIKELY THUNDERBOLT

The young man sat alone behind a pile of large crates in the corner of the public square. He buried his head in his arms, trying to hide the tears that poured forth. He had never before felt such humiliation. Though he could not see them, he heard the Assembly members passing by, and their words stung bitterly.

"Have you ever before in your life heard such a tortured speech?" There was a burst of laughter, and then another voice replied, "The *raws* of the *rand* require *arr peopre*—" Fresh guffaws made it impossible to hear what followed.

When the laughter had died down, the first voice continued, "If you can't even pronounce simple words, what makes you think you can win a legal suit defending yourself?"

The voices grew distant, but the young man's embarrassment remained acute. Orphaned in his childhood and left with a large fortune, he had been forced to watch in dismay as his would-be guardians squandered his wealth. Once he came of age, he swore to himself, he would stand in his own defense and win back what had been stolen from him! But that dream was in jeopardy, as he wondered whether he ever dared approach the Assembly again after such a failed attempt.

A stick poked his side, and he glanced up in surprise. "It wasn't *that* bad." An elderly man, one of the Athenian Assembly members, stood over him. A gentle smile lit the old man's face. The young boy quickly wiped his face with the backs of his hands. His throat was too tight to speak.

The elderly man continued, "You know, your diction is very much like that of Pericles. I wouldn't give up so easily, my friend."

The youth's eyes opened wide. "You really think so?"

The older man nodded. "I do. That doesn't mean you don't have a long way to go. But I think you some ability. With real effort and good training, you might do all right for yourself." The elderly man went on his way, but those words, spoken in passing, fueled a fire of talent and discipline that grew so bright, its influence would shine throughout the world.

That stuttering youth, Demosthenes, would become perhaps the greatest orator of the ancient world and one of the best the world has ever known. His influence would grow to inspire Cicero, Juvenal, and Henry Clay, among others, shaping everything from Cicero's own attacks against Mark Antony to the Federalist Papers. But his influence came by great effort.

Rather than dwell on his speech impediment and his obvious unnatural style of delivery, Demosthenes turned wholeheartedly to improving himself in the thing he loved to do: speaking. He studied great writers and speakers, and spent much time improving his diction, voice, and gestures. All day he would practice and on into the night. In later years, when asked what the three most important oratory elements were, he replied, "Delivery, delivery, and delivery!"[3] Lucian, an ancient rhetorician, once saw eight beautifully bound copies of Thucydides, all written in Demosthenes' own hand, showing the intensity of his efforts to improve his learning and oratorical abilities.

His discipline paid off. At the age of twenty, he argued effectively in court, gaining what was left of his inheritance and opening the door for a career in oratory that would touch the entire world. His studies also fueled a love of freedom that would inspire his fellow Athenians and cost him his life.

Demosthenes' career as an orator began at almost the same time that Philip II of Macedon ascended the throne. Demosthenes devoted his best years and efforts to opposing Macedon's expansion and defending Athenian democracy. Throughout his life the freedom, laws, and morals of Athens were under siege by Macedonian rulers; first Philip, then Alexander, and finally Antipater attacked the once great city-state. Over and over again, despite loss after loss, Demosthenes encouraged his countrymen to fight for their liberties and to resist the subjugation by Macedon that would surely result in the loss of democracy and of liberty.

His views were far from popular among some Athenian elite; they were also extremely costly. Though the Athenians occasionally won a skirmish against their bigger, wealthier opponents, the Macedonians consistently overcame Athens and her allies in battle and often at great cost in lives. That Demosthenes was still able to encourage his countrymen to continue the fight speaks to his well-developed gifts of persuasion and reason and his deep yearning to inspire them to value liberty and democracy.

Demosthenes was not content to see Athens, alone, oppose their mighty foe. Although an unpopular move, he travelled to surrounding city-states, arguing that it would be "better to die a thousand deaths" than pay homage to Macedon.[4] He urged Athenians to cherish the values that had made Athenian democracy and Athenian life what it once had been and to eschew the corruption that was beginning to overwhelm the city. It was impossible, he argued, "to gain permanent power by injustice, perjury and falsehood." Just as a ship or house gains its chief strength from its substructure, he said, so "too in affairs of state the principles and foundations must be truth and justice."[5]

Plutarch later remarked on Demosthenes' constancy, observing that "the same party and post in politics which he held from the beginning, to these he kept constant to the end; and was so far from leaving them while he lived, that he chose rather to forsake his life than his purpose."[6] Indeed, when Antipater, Alexander's successor, sought the life of Demosthenes, the great orator chose to end his own life as an act of sealing his words and deeds for all time rather than surrender to his enemy.

The once-stammering youth, through determined effort and a passion for liberty, became a "blazing thunderbolt"[7] and a standard-bearer for all those who carry the torch of freedom forward.

LESSONS FROM DEMOSTHENES ON HOW TO PASS THE TORCH

1. Weaknesses aren't excuses for failure; they're invitations to success. Demosthenes didn't choose the easy path. He paid the price to become the best in his field, paving the way for others who see the importance of carrying the torch of freedom onward through time.

2. Liberty inspires. One of Demosthenes' greatest strengths was his ability to inspire his fellow countrymen around the truth that freedom was worth fighting for. Fellow orators were less influential; their pragmatic focus on colluding with the Macedonians was neither moving nor meaningful.

3. Democracy requires that laws be followed by everyone, without exception. Demosthenes argued adamantly that democratic states will fail if the rule of law is manipulated by those who pursue power and control.

CHAPTER 6

THE RELUCTANT DEMIGOD

"We have the report!" The young soldier was breathless, having just returned from scoping the enemy's troops.

"What have you learned?" The general was clean-shaven, making him appear even younger than his thirty-four years.

"The enemy has over four thousand cavalry, and—we esti-mate—over thirty-five thousand troops." The soldier swallowed hard. "That's not all—we counted at least eighty elephants, trained for war. We're outnumbered, that's for sure."

The general was calm. He quietly thanked the young man. "You may go."

He sat on the edge of his bed, stroking his chin and speaking to himself. "The undefeated Carthaginian and the undefeated Roman meet again. Neither willing to accept defeat." He paused and then continued, "I have a promise to keep."

The quiet before the battle often made him introspective. Since before he was born, his family had fought against Carthaginian domination. He could hardly count all the friends and family who had given their lives to the conflict. From the time of Hannibal's first assault on Rome, one fifth of all Roman military-age men had died in the conflict with Carthage—including his father-in-law, his uncle, and even his father.

He shook his head, remembering his last words to his father. He had promised him to continue the struggle against Carthage his entire life, if necessary. "Not again, Hannibal, not again!" he said, shaking his fist.

At the battle of Cannae, when he was just a youth, his countrymen had suffered terrible losses at the hands of Hannibal. He remembered hearing, with sinking heart, that in the face of such loss many Roman politicians were about to surrender Rome to Hannibal. Struck with courage and conviction, he had gathered his friends. They stormed the meeting, swords in hand, and forced everyone present to swear their allegiance and continued faithfulness to Rome. That felt so long ago. Would today be the day—the day he would put Carthaginian domination and oppression behind himself and his countrymen forever?

Since leading his first Roman troops in battle at age twenty-five, he had never lost a battle. He didn't intend to lose today either. If he won this battle, the entire western Mediterranean would be under his control. He shook his head again: failure today was not an option.

He walked swiftly from his tent. "Gather the men!" he called out. Traditional battle formation was to spread troops equally, three horizontal lines deep. But this was no traditional battle. "Form perpendicular lines! Set the traps!" He commanded. "Trumpeters at the front!"

Hannibal's troops arrived in opposition, elephants in front—but something was wrong. Rather than the elephants mowing down soldiers in horizontal lines and exposing the enemy's flanks, as

Hannibal had planned, the elephants were met first by traps, than by trumpeters, both causing confusion and panic among the large beasts. Once some semblance of order was regained, the elephants were goaded sideways along the perpendicular lines of soldiers, rather than *through* them. Sharp spears and javelins pierced their sides, causing many of the elephants to turn back and charge their own ranks. By day's end the Romans had won a decisive victory at Zama over the Carthaginians, in what was later called the "Roman Cannae."

Scipio Africanus, statesman and soldier, refused the normal spoils of war and conquest. In typical Scipio-fashion and against expectation and tradition, he did not victoriously raze the conquered city. Nor did he kill or humiliate the Carthaginian general, Hannibal. On the contrary, he allowed Hannibal to retain civic leadership of Carthage, and his terms were so light that Carthage was ensured a quick return to full prosperity.

Scipio, perhaps the greatest general of all time, fought whole-heartedly not just against the Carthaginians, who sought to conquer and force all those around them to subjugation; he also fought against the typical corruption and traditions of his day. Because of Scipio's success, the torch of freedom would continue to spread Greek culture, Christianity, and ultimately Western civilization.

When Scipio returned to Rome, he refused the honors that others would have happily awarded him, Consul for Life and even Dictator. He sought no political power, insisting that the act of winning that great battle of Zama was its own reward, and he would accept no other.

He was a master of military strategy, evident not only in how he raised and trained his troops but also how he led them during and after war. After one battle, he was brought a beautiful young woman from the conquered city. He learned she was engaged to be married, and he insisted she be returned to her betrothed, along with the ransom money her parents had offered for her safe return. These and other stories demonstrate his unique leadership perspectives and characteristic mercy and strength.

Scipio successfully defended the Roman Republic against Carthage, allowing Rome to enter the peak of its Republic period. Like Cincinnatus before him and George Washington long after, he surrendered his military and political power in favor of an agricultural life, yearning not for riches and honor but for the quiet and peace of his rural home and the freedom of his countrymen.

LESSONS FROM SCIPIO ON HOW TO PASS THE TORCH

1. Freedom fighters are not fueled by popularity and power. They wield the sword of influence and prestige on behalf of their countrymen and willingly relinquish it when it's time for them to move on.

2. Scipio did not draw his allegiance across strict "party lines," treating with respect and decency only those he admired and aligned with. He saw the wisdom and power that came from being thoughtful, fair, and even generous toward everyone, foe and friend alike.

3. Bondage comes in many forms—one of which attempts to limit others' freedom through conquest. Scipio passed the torch of freedom by bravely resisting this type of bondage for himself and his countrymen, paving the way for others to carry on the torch for generations to come.

CHAPTER 7

THE MENTOR OF THINKING MEN

The sun had set hours ago; one dim candle lit the room, but the man at the desk seemed not to notice the darkness. Piles of books surrounded him, on the floor, on the desk, even on the bed. One well-worn volume lay open in front of him, and his fingers traced the words carefully.

His hair was disheveled and his clothes unkempt. His eyes, wet with tears, shone brightly. The edges of his mouth were turned upward in exultation. With trembling hand, he set his pen to the paper and began to write.

> Your letters I sought for long and diligently; and finally, where I least expected it, I found them. At once I read them, over and over, with the utmost eagerness.... I long had known how excellent a guide you have proved for others; at last I was to learn what sort of guidance you gave yourself.
>
> Now it is your turn to be the listener. Hearken, wherever you are, to the words of advice, or rather of sorrow and regret, that fall, not unaccompanied by tears, from the lips

of one of your successors, who loves you faithfully and cherishes your name. O spirit ever restless and perturbed![8]

Who had inspired such ardent words of admiration? What worthy soul deserved such praise? The author of the letter was the Italian scholar and poet Petrarch, and his subject was the unequalled Cicero. Petrarch's discovery of the great Roman orator's works is said to have launched the Renaissance, which one author described as being "really the revival of Cicero."[9]

Long had Petrarch studied the great statesman, Marcus Tullius Cicero, the Roman philosopher, politician, lawyer, and political theorist; the incomparable consul, constitutionalist, linguist, translator, and renowned orator. Long had he admired Cicero's philosophical views aimed at political efficacy; long had he considered Cicero's impact on those who followed, including Augustine, Boethius, and Lactantius (and through the latter, also Constantine.)

These and others studied and admired Cicero for good reason. His works have particular relevance to any student of liberty. This key torchbearer contributed to freedom and its preservation in essential ways, both during his lifetime and through his written legacy impacting generations that followed him.

Cicero was born to a respectable Roman family who were part of the equestrian class. By the age of fifteen, he was already well versed in both Greek and Latin. He studied literature, law, and philosophy and spent much time improving his writing and speaking abilities through a variety of oratorical exercises. By age twenty-five, he began his own law practice, and he continued his education as he traveled throughout Greece and the eastern Mediterranean.

Ever the defender of liberty, he fought off attacks against it both at home and abroad. As he traveled, he spread the ideas he had studied, and it has been written of him in modern times that his long-ago travels and knowledge positioned him to be "the great transmitter of Stoic ideas from Greece to Rome, [helping] shape the great structures of Roman law which became pervasive in Western civilization."[10]

When he was Roman Consul and conspirators sought to overthrow Rome, Cicero had them executed immediately. Later, when Gaius Julius Caesar's dictatorship further threatened the foundations of Roman liberty, Cicero championed a return to traditional republican government and was a staunch defender of that type of government.

He advocated the idea that government is a trustee of the people, morally obligated to serve society, not itself. By extension of that principle, he argued, society is something larger than government and separate from it. He reasoned vehemently that a key role of government was to protect private property, not public officials' coffers. And as Rome continued to deteriorate, both politically and economically, Cicero's voice continued to rise in opposition to the decay and corruption he saw daily increasing.

He warned that at no other time was Rome so deeply in debt; never before had the electorate given so much sway to corruption and bribery, selling their votes to the highest bidder. He stood on unwavering principles, courageously denouncing tyranny and fighting for liberty at the cost of his own life. He felt his political career was his most important achievement, and when he refused to concede his strongly opposed political views, he was executed—beheaded—by imperial decree of the Second Triumvirate.

Cicero left a wealth of writings and a legacy of ideas that would shape those who followed in dramatic ways. He has been called

the greatest influence on European literature, bar none;[11] he intro-
duced the chief schools of Greek philosophy; and his works rank
among the most influential in all of European culture. His writings
on the last days of the Roman Republic provide key insight into
that historical period, and his observations on important principles of freedom had a major effect on the later writings of Locke,
Hume, and Montesquieu, all intellectual heavyweights and cham-
pions of freedom.

Those concerned with freedom today must know and understand the lessons of liberty taught long ago by Cicero, once a
household name. His message speaks powerfully "from the dust"
to those who have inherited a threatened freedom, and his words
written long ago could not more perfectly pertain to those wishing
to carry the torch of freedom today:

> Long before our time the customs of our ancestors
> molded admirable men, and in turn those eminent men
> upheld the ways and institutions of their forebears. Our
> age, however, inherited the Republic as if it were some beau-
> tiful painting of bygone ages, its colors fading through great
> antiquity; and not only has our time neglected to freshen the
> colors of the picture, but we have failed to preserve its form
> and outline.

Voltaire perhaps said it best: "Cicero taught us how to think."
We are remiss if we hope to defend liberty without understanding
how to think. We must not fail to take the opportunity to learn
how to think from that great Roman orator himself.

LESSONS FROM CICERO ON HOW TO PASS THE TORCH

1. History repeats itself; freedom depends on knowing the cycles of history and learning from them. Today's political decay and economic instability were also experienced long ago by ancient Rome. Cicero saw these same conditions and wrote insightfully on why they come about and how to reverse them. Rome reflects in many key ways our current situation today, including:

    a. Economic expansion leading to a world empire dependent on lower wage earners with low living standards;

    b. Economic downturn, leading to unemployment;

    c. Lower class increasingly influenced by demagogic politicians;

    d. Upper class with almost unrestricted power; and

    e. Abnormally inflated costs of grain and other goods necessary to livelihood.[1]

2. The influence of statesmen is spread and sustained by the preservation of their ideas. Torchbearers read the works of those who have gone before and create their own written works for those who follow them.

3. Torchbearers must stand for their principles—even and especially when it costs them greatly, including their own lives.

CHAPTER 8

THE ROMAN CONSUL WHO DESPISED ROME

The senator stood with eyes aflame, one hand raised high, the other holding his prepared speech. He did not glance down, as he seemed to know the words by heart. His audience listened attentively, some enraptured by his words, others shifting uncomfortably in their seats and glancing furtively around. They knew his words were not popular among some senators, and though he held high position, not all agreed with his inflammatory oration.

The man's voice was quiet but piercing. "And that tyrant Domitian—he did much to destroy our once great Republic! Agricola, esteemed general and my own father-in-law, was scarcely spared during that tyrant's reign. Domitian, who left no interval, no breathing space—as if with one continuous blow—drained the lifeblood of this, our commonwealth!"

His voice began to rise, and those listening were reminded, once more, why this man was considered one of the best orators Rome had ever produced. "Not long did we wait before our hands dragged that great statesman Helvidius to prison; not long before we gazed on the dying looks of Manricus and Rusticus, once consuls, praetors, and friends to the Republic; not long, before we were steeped in Senecio's innocent blood!" Heads nodded in remembrance of the lost lives of those innocent statesmen who had been sacrificed for the cause of the empire.

"The worst part of our miseries was to see and be seen, and to know that our sighs were being recorded!" With even greater vehemence he ended his speech: "To ravage, to slaughter, to usurp, under false titles, they call empire; and where they make a desert, they call it peace."[13]

He stepped down from his lectern, his countrymen cheering him on. Long had their country been rent by disorder, inequality, and injustice. Long had the innocent been trodden upon by those seeking glory and eminence. But would it ever change?

Much remains unknown about that great Roman orator, Tacitus. We do not know where he was born or in what year. We know little of his family and nothing of his death. But there is much reason to study what we do know about him and to learn from his writings. The time in which he lived mirrored many of today's circumstances, and the United States founders not only knew his name well but studied his works with great interest and care.

Tacitus provides an important firsthand record of the early first century. His writings are the most reliable source of history for that period. It is from Tacitus that we learn about the declining culture and loss of leadership endemic to this period of the Roman Empire.

Tacitus stood witness to a period in time when the Roman Republic was no more. The democratic-republic principles of government that had once been espoused gave way to first kings and then emperors, complete with expanding influence, and tax increases necessary to support the growing government's programs and corruption. These taxes, Tacitus testified, quickly became burdensome, and civil wars began to break out across the empire. The borders were especially dangerous and volatile as Rome attempted to control her neighbors and expand her influence, while those she attempted to dominate resisted and resented her control.

Turmoil became the order of the day, with conflict found throughout the empire. Some resisted more successfully than others, and Britain developed its own method of resistance. Composed of fiercely independent factions, British tribes organized themselves in a kind of democratic tribal culture, in efforts to fend off the invading Romans. They also developed improved methods of communication, allowing various tribes to transmit important information related to resistance.

The Romans, in turn, capitalized on the economic-based culture they found in London. To calm and control the barbarian communities, the Romans built theaters, public baths, circuses, and amphitheaters for Roman-style games and shows. "Step by step," wrote Tacitus, "they were led to things which dispose to vice, the lounge, the bath, the elegant banquet. All this in their ignorance they called civilization, when it was but a part of their servitude."[14]

Tacitus also witnessed the repression of certain religious groups for the sake of entertainment and explained of some early Christian martyrs that "they were destroyed, not for the public good, but to gratify the cruelty of an individual [Nero]."

America's founders valued the observations of Tacitus because they saw many parallels between the spread and decline of Rome and the world powers and patterns that existed in their day. Their studies of these early philosophers, historians, and statesmen gave them courage to face the challenges of their time and clarity about how to overcome them successfully. Thomas Jefferson once wrote, "I read one or two newspapers a week, but with reluctance give even that time from Tacitus and Homer and so much agreeable reading. I feel a much greater interest in knowing what has happened two or three thousand years ago, than in what is passing now."

How does the shift from republic to empire occur? Why do people turn a blind eye as injustice and corruption become the order of the day? How can great leaders be educated and found who are fit to lead a nation in a time of crisis?

These questions are not new; they are as old as time. They are questions considered by Tacitus of old as well as great statesmen and women of all ages. They are worth asking again, and the effort of looking to those earlier torchbearers for lessons and answers will be richly repaid.

LESSONS FROM TACITUS ON HOW TO PASS THE TORCH

1. Empire affords a degree of peace and security for which many people are willing to sacrifice freedom. As Tacitus observed, the price for empire is steep and always involves surrendering freedom.

2. As government grows, the taxes necessary to support it likewise increase. As taxes increase, the middle class collapses and laws that favor the financial manipulators multiply.

3. Culture is a powerful tool for preserving or destroying liberty. Arts and entertainment have great power to shape the morals and ideals of a civilization.

PART II

THE RISE OF CHRISTIANITY

As in life, so in history, progress often takes three steps forward and then two steps back. The preservation of liberty requires constant vigilance and determined effort. While it is hard to overstate the impact on freedom of the contributions of Greece and Rome, neither civilization lasted long under democratic forms of government. Something was still missing from liberty's equation, and the flame of liberty burned only briefly in those early city-states.

Greece lasted less than two hundred years as a democracy. Rome lasted about twice that long as a republic, although her common people enjoyed relative freedom for a much shorter period as wealthy individuals began to corrupt her laws. Time gnawed slowly but surely away at the Roman Republic until republican principles gave way to empire, and with it the first great experiment with republicanism disappeared. Slowly but surely, power, land, and wealth were again wrested from the common people back into the hands of the few.

For Rome's first hundred years, all Roman citizens recognized the importance of law. Citizenship was highly valued, and participation in government was seen as a privilege and an important right. But then a variety of influences began to factionalize her inhabitants and cut away at both respect for law and involved citizenship.

Imperial expansion spread Roman law far beyond its original borders but could not likewise spread an appreciation for that same law. Electoral methods that worked on a small scale were corrupted and manipulated on a large scale, striking at the roots of liberty. Most important, there was no common view of people's moral obligations. Doing what was right was replaced with the idea of acting according to individual rights, as defined by each individual. If something increased one's power, it was good; it was bad if it decreased one's power. Power was the ultimate rod by which to measure one's actions, while citizenship and honoring the law fell by the wayside. Of course liberty suffered as a result.

Today, we see this same attack on the roots of our liberty. Appreciation for and adherence to an inner moral compass, essential for liberty, are under attack, and those who claim a moral high ground for their actions are ridiculed in public and private.

The flame of liberty burned dimly and then finally went out when the Roman Republic formally ended following Caesar's legendary "crossing of the Rubicon." In this rebellious act,

Caesar crossed the legal boundary of Rome, entering territory where he was forbidden to pass. After years of battles, Caesar became sole ruler of Rome but enjoyed that position only briefly before he was assassinated by an elite group of senators.

The cycle of war and intrigue continued: those with power sought for more, offering as a sacrifice for increased power the lives and liberties of the ignorant masses. In killing Caesar, the Roman senators hoped to wrest power and property from his hands and secure it for themselves. Civil war erupted following Caesar's death, ending in Octavian's return to Rome and his ascension to the throne as Augustus ("Exalted One"), marking the end of the Republic. The Romans, no longer unified by republican principles or any common ideal, struggled through more than two centuries for unity and direction.

The birth, life, and death of Christ, along with the subsequent rise of Christianity, brought about some important changes that directly impacted liberty's potential and influence. While the Greeks and Romans had been in a sense highly religious, offering prayers and performing rituals to household gods, their religion offered no unifying moral code to strengthen and sustain the growing empire.

Constantine the Great, who rose to power in AD 293, recognized the absence of unity and shared vision among those belonging to the Roman Empire. What could unite people over such a vast territory and with such varied beliefs? Constantine found in the Christian faith the power to unify his subjects. Religion served as a convenient way to direct and unite the masses and an effective mechanism for enforcing the idea that God willed those in power to be so. Thus, he firmly established the idea that to threaten those in power was to displease God.

Incidentally, by bolstering the power and authority of the Catholic church (catholic meaning "universal," precisely what he hoped his empire would become), Constantine at the same time struck at the roots of classical text and thought. The rise of ancient Christianity marked a concurrent loss of appreciation for and fluency in Greek and Roman ideas and texts, and the flame of liberty was extinguished for a time. Not for another thousand years would those ideas again be revisited.

Constantine's decision to blend political power with Christian principles and influence would set the tone for Europe and Western Asia for the next millennium, until an invention by an unknown, unrecognized German blacksmith next revolutionized the world, and the flame of liberty leapt once more to life.

CHAPTER 9

THE GREAT ENCOURAGER

The group of men stood in a close circle, talking in hushed tones. Christ's death had surprised and confused them, but the resurrected Lord's appearance had brought assurance and made clear their mandate. Still, it was no easy task to take the glad news to places and people who were often unwelcoming and even hostile. This strange turn of events required great caution; they each knew their lives could be at stake.

A tall man spoke up. "Tell us again what you've heard; don't leave anything out."

A shorter man replied, "It happened to Saul, the Pharisee and persecutor of Christians. He was sent by the high priest here in Jerusalem to the officials in Damascus. He has authority to bind every new believer and bring them to Jerusalem for punishment."

The listeners' faces were grim. "They say"—he paused, scanning their faces, then continued—"they say that on the road to Damascus he was stopped by an angel. He is now a believer."

The tall man shook his head in disbelief. "Go on," he urged his friend.

"Once the Jewish leaders heard of it, they sought his life. But a few days ago he escaped, in a basket lowered over the walls of the city, and now *he is here! In Jerusalem!*"

The tall man again shook his head. "It's a trick," he said matter-of-factly. Most of the men nodded in agreement. "Avoid him at all costs, and if you hear word of where he is, inform the rest of us. We must be on our guard."

His eyes caught those of a Cypriot who stood in the corner of the room. "Understand? He's not safe."

The man in the corner replied softly. "There was a time when I too was an unbeliever. What if the report is true? What if he is on our side?"

The tall man stared, incredulous, and then replied, "If you wish to risk your life, go ahead. Remember Stephen, who was stoned?" A hush fell on the room. "Saul was there. Did he save Stephen? No, quite the contrary. And if you don't listen to my words, you may be next."

The tall man left the room, and the others slowly followed. But the man in the corner remained, thoughtfully pondering what he would do. He didn't ponder long. He also went out and approached a nearby shop.

"Excuse me," he asked the shopkeeper. "I've heard there was here yesterday a man by the name of Saul, come from Jerusalem...." He didn't need to finish his inquiry.

The shopkeeper nodded. "Yes, he was here again this morning. He went that way." He nodded in the direction of the marketplace.

The man swallowed hard. "Thank you," he said. He walked quickly in the direction the shopkeeper had indicated and soon saw a small crowd gathered. A man was speaking before the group. The topic made it clear: this was Saul.

The Cypriot believer approached him from behind, and Saul turned in surprise. "Saul, I am Barnabas, a believer in Christ. Will you tell me your story?"

Barnabas, the "son of encouragement,"[15] was never one to be turned away by unpolished words or unusual believers. He was the first in Jerusalem to befriend Paul, and after seeking him out, he brought Paul to the other apostles, who eventually realized that Paul's conversion was, indeed, sincere. Barnabas welcomed Paul to the fold of believers and thus paved the way for Paul's important mission and contributions to the New Testament.

Barnabas again demonstrated his openness and clear-headed equity when he was sent to investigate the first instance of Jews and Greeks worshipping together. The incident caused quite some consternation, and Barnabas was sent to ascertain the situation. Rather than critique the group of worshippers, he listened openly. When he saw what he called the grace of God among the group of believers, he rejoiced.

When Barnabas began his outreach to the Gentiles in Antioch, he recognized that Paul's gifts of persuasion and conviction would be of great benefit. He again sought Paul out and asked for his assistance in Antioch, creating one of the most influential missionary teams of the Christian faith.

Barnabas served not only as a steadfast support and companion to Paul, even before Paul's influence was appreciated, but also as a mentor. John Mark, another apostle, accompanied Barnabas and Paul on their early missions. However, John Mark left the two to serve alone after some kind of falling out. Later, John Mark wished to rejoin the elders, but after a sharp contention[16] between Paul and John Mark, the two men were again at odds.

It appears that Paul was ready for greater leadership, as was John Mark, neither of whom could properly grow and lead out together. In response, Barnabas created two missionary teams: Paul and a new companion taking one path and Barnabas and John Mark continuing together. Barnabas's mentorship of John Mark also seemed to lead to a reconciliation of the trio, evidenced by Paul's writings while a prisoner in Rome: "John Mark...[has] been a comfort to me."[17]

In many ways Barnabas, the great encourager, served as a behind-the-scenes mentor for others, seeking out and assisting those in need and supporting the cause of Christianity in fundamental, sincere ways.

Perhaps no other underground historical leader can be credited with so much and yet have so little written and recorded of him; nevertheless, his impact was profound. Freedom rests on servant-leaders like Barnabas, who courageously pay it forward and mentor and befriend those around them.

LESSONS FROM BARNABAS ON HOW TO PASS THE TORCH

1. Building relationships and influencing both those like and unlike us is a skill that torchbearers must possess. If we can only relate to and appreciate those like us, our influence will spread no further than those who already embody the ideals we proclaim.

2. Community building, not factionalizing, builds stronger societies and connections able to stand the test of time. Barnabas focused on the strengths of those he associated with and led, which allowed him to connect people in meaningful ways and repair broken relationships.

CHAPTER 10

THE FATHER OF CHURCH HISTORY

The bishop slipped around a corner. He stepped into the recess of a doorway, tucked back in a narrow passageway. His breathing was heavy from the chase. He glanced upward, grateful for the cloud cover that made the night even darker. His heart pounded so loudly he could not discern if the footsteps he heard were pounding towards him—or away. He held his breath, though his lungs burned. *Please*, he silently prayed, *please keep me hidden*.

He heard shouting, and more footsteps, and then the night grew quiet. Minutes passed, but he dared not move. If he were wrong and the steps had not passed but were waiting for him somewhere out there, that would be the end of things. His legs began to shake from fatigue—he was certainly malnourished, and the prison walls had offered little room for movement on the rare occasions he had had enough energy to walk about. The prison guards would certainly come back looking for him, and he must find a better spot to hide. But where?

Thunder shook the skies, and raindrops began to pour down. He glanced upward at the darkness, despair filling his heart. Then he noticed something—a mound of empty crates, piled high against the side of a nearby building. If he could make room for himself among the crates…as long as they didn't fall and crush him, they would provide the perfect hiding spot. Soon he had buried himself among the boxes, and though the rain easily found its way through the cracks and drenched him, it didn't keep him from drifting off to sleep.

"What do we have here?" The booming voice shook him awake, his heart leaping to his throat. He was done for. He looked up to see the round, red face of a fisherman, who was laughing loudly. The man bent his head close to the bishop's and said in a hushed voice, "Today's catch, fresh Christian if I am not wrong!"

The bishop's eyes were wide. "I heard they had an escapee last night. But don't worry, man. I'm no Christian, but the things they've been heaping on them folk, it's not right." The kindly fisherman straightened up, looking both ways, and said, "Follow me."

He led the bishop to a nearby home. "Stay here till things quiet down," he said. "The fresh air never hurt anybody, but Diocletian won't treat you well if he finds you out there. It's better to stay indoors for a while."

"Thank you, thank you!" whispered the bishop.

"No word! I'll be back later tonight, but help yourself to whatever I have."

Again the bishop thanked the fisherman, and then joined the departing fisherman by the door.

"Please, sir, I've had no news in prison and only escaped last night. Can you tell me anything of Pamphilus?"

The fisherman's face clouded. "He's no more, friend. Him and the whole lot who were with him, martyred."

The bishop was filled with disbelief, "No," he said. "Oh no, not Pamphilus.... Since I was twenty-five, I have studied at his side," the bishop explained, tears streaming down his face.

"I'm sorry," offered the fisherman, but after a moment he added, "I need to go."

The bishop nodded and then spoke up once more. "And his books? Pamphilus' library—it was burned?" He choked the words out. The books passed on by Origen, carefully guarded by his mentor, Pamphilus...the bishop himself had helped gather and painstakingly document all of the Christian writings and records for the last three hundred years.

"I do not know," the fisherman said simply. "Seems that's what they usually do, burn everything, but I don't know." The fisherman stepped outside, and then turned around before closing the door behind him. "What is your name?" he asked.

"Eusebius." The fisherman nodded and was gone.

Eusebius slowly, secretly made his way to Caesarea, where the library of Pamphilus had been stored. He took great care to avoid being known. Diocletian had once sent a messenger to ask the oracles how to treat the Christians. The messenger had returned and reported, "Persecute them all." Diocletian did not fail the supposed mandate, and his reign was accompanied by the worst persecution of Christians in all the time that Rome ruled the world.

Eusebius, though broken over the loss of his great mentor and friend, did not allow self-pity and grief to rule his world. As have great men and women throughout all time, he forged in those difficult circumstances a stronger character and greater desire to succeed.

He became known as the father of church history for his tireless efforts gathering, editing and compiling historical documents. He wrote extensive chronologies, including a history of martyrs, treatises, apologetic works, and records defending the Christian faith. His crowning work, his *Ecclesiastical History of the Church*, is the first surviving history of the Christian church. As with any documentation of its magnitude, it is not without controversy. However, its merits far outweigh its faults, and it is an excellent help for anyone deepening their biblical research.

Eusebius was well educated and well connected. When Constantine, the first Christian Roman emperor, assumed power, Eusebius enjoyed the great emperor's favor and served him as a prominent adviser. Upon Constantine's death, he wrote a panegyric eulogizing him.

Eusebius witnessed the worst of Christian persecution; he participated in the First Council of Nicaea; and he read and reviewed more early Christian history than perhaps any other person. By doing so, he kept alive the story of this important period, illuminating an important time that would otherwise be lost in the darkness of the past.

LESSONS FROM EUSEBIUS ON HOW TO PASS THE TORCH

1. History repeats itself; freedom depends on knowing the cycles of history and learning from them. Eusebius and historians like him enable those who follow to learn from those stories and cycles by studying their works.

2. Leaders typically stand on the shoulders of someone else. Eusebius benefited greatly from the works of Origen and Pamphilus before him. They paved the way for him to compile his own history of Christianity, which he certainly could not have done without their efforts and preparation.

CHAPTER 11

THE EMPEROR-APOSTLE

It was exhilarating—the thought that east and west were finally reunited under one emperor! It had taken many years and cost many lives, but this time things had fallen in his favor.

The new emperor thought back on the previous year. It had begun when, on another excursion, he had crossed into his enemy Licinius' territory, the territory of "the west." Licinius had reacted with great hostility. In response, the battle-worn emperor of the east had decided the time had come to try again—to try to wrest the western powers from Licinius and unite both empires, east and west, under one ruler: himself!

They met at the Hebrus River, neither side anxious to cross the river and risk encountering the enemy on unfair ground. But when his enemy showed no sign of moving, he designed a stratagem. "There, and there!" he pointed down the river only a stone's throw from the opposing troops. "Prepare ropes and bridge materials!"

The enemy watched confidently. If a river crossing were attempted there, they were sure of victory. They could easily descend on their enemies and handily slaughter them. Day followed day as the bridge conspicuously began to materialize and the ropes grew in length. But at night, unbeknownst to Licinius and his troops, the emperor quietly prepared a second crossing, in the opposite direction, hidden by a wooded hillside. Finally all was ready, and their surprise nighttime attack resulted in a massacre. It struck an important blow on his enemy's forces and pride.

Not long afterwards the forces met again, this time near Byzantium. In the narrow waters of the Hellespont, Licinius suffered terrible defeat and thereafter withdrew his troops to the safety of the city. In hot pursuit the eastern emperor followed Licinius northward. He made the first move against Licinius after withdrawing to his tent.

He prayed and received an answer. It was time to act. "Raise the standard!" he called. The standard showed in broad display the characters Chi-Rho—the first two Greek letters representing Christ's name.

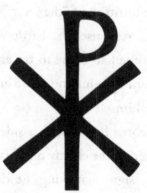

His enemy Licinius, he knew, had grown to fear this standard. In fact, Licinius forbade his troops from attacking it or even gazing upon it. The enemy had their own standards—flags painted with images of the pagan gods of Rome. The eastern emperor made no secret of his advance this time. He ordered a direct frontal attack and a second slaughter ensued, this time resulting in decisive victory. Though Licinius escaped, the emperor was content in knowing his position was secure: Gaius Flavius Valerius Aurelius Constantinus Augustus—Emperor Constantine, of east *and* west!

Preceding Constantine's reign the Roman Empire had begun facing serious decline. Contentious factions and unscrupulous officials had broken the public spirit. Widespread malaise was the order of the day, resulting from broken promises and inefficient political systems. The economy in turn began to stagnate. The income of the once productive empire proved insufficient to support the heavy taxes, demands of a growing populace and increasing corruption. Hyperinflation led to currency manipulation. Prices skyrocketed, and class war escalated.

In addition, Diocletian's brutal measures against the Christians resulted in the loss of churches, scriptures, and the treasures stored within those churches. Christians were burned, beaten, tortured, branded, hanged, and decapitated—often for no reason other than a means of entertainment.

Constantine had observed, however, that despite the persecution, the number of Christians only seemed to grow. Non-Christians were horrified by the treatment of the Christians they observed and sometimes joined them out of admiration. The harder Diocletian fought to exterminate them, the more fervently Christians believed, and the greater their numbers became.

Two events brought merciful relief to the Christians. First, Diocletian surrendered his throne, and second, Constantine himself converted to the Christian faith. The night before a key battle he had a dream wherein Christ visited him. He recalled seeing a cross in the noonday sun, inscribed with the Greek words, "By this, conquer."

Ever after he carried the cross into battle as a standard, soon after reuniting east and west, he sent forth the Edict of Milan, granting all Christians religious toleration. According to Eusebius, as a result of the edict, "the whole human race was freed from the oppression of the tyrants.... [W]e especially, who had fixed our hopes upon the Christ of God, had gladness unspeakable."[18]

These experiences and others contributed to Constantine's feeling that he was himself a type of apostle of the Christian church, spreading and defending the word of Christ, just as did the earliest apostles.

After conquering Licinius and capturing Byzantium, Constantine moved quickly to reposition the government seat to East Byzantium, renaming the area Constantinople. This move had several advantages. It was located in a favorable geographic position and offered many economic benefits including ease of trade. He could control the sea routes of the east, while maintaining his influence in the west. Finally, the new capital allowed a mix of Greek, Roman, and Eastern cultural and economic influences.

During this period Constantine became a great patron of the arts and one of the most memorable builders in the history of Rome and the world. He founded an architectural revolution, attracting scholars and artists from throughout the world.

The unity that Constantine hoped and fought for did not last long, however. Rivalries between the popes of Rome and the patriarchs of Constantinople occurred. Eventually a separation took place between the eastern and western parts of the church, and the

Roman unity that had existed for more than five hundred years came to an end, followed by the final collapse of Rome in AD 476.

The fall of the Roman Empire left a void of order, and a new system called feudalism began to replace the republican systems and ideals that had once held sway. At the same time Christianity rose in popularity, and in the century following Constantine the number of Christians rose from an estimated five million to thirty million.

Constantine lived during a time of great wars and revolutions; he founded a new empire and paved the way for Christianity to spread throughout the world. The events that surrounded his birth and death offer rich history lessons about the rise and fall of nations, lessons with many parallels to our own day.

LESSONS FROM CONSTANTINE ON HOW TO PASS THE TORCH

1. Christianity is not as openly attacked today as it was before the Edict of Milan. Nevertheless it is still threatened by the undertones of modernism and relativism that permeate American media and educational systems. Christianity is cast in a negative light and portrayed as an invalid belief option. Recognizing these quiet attacks and responding to them with courage and clarity is key to protecting religious and political freedom.

2. Constantinople eventually fell due to controversies, scandals, and corruption. We face similar challenges today. Learning about the events of history allows us to have a better chance of influencing future events in positive ways and allows us to pass on important lessons to future generations.

3. Constantinople remained until its fall to the Turks in 1453, ending what scholars call one of the four golden ages in history. This period offers rich examples of scandals, controversy, and corruption similar to today. It's worth studying in order to preserve the torch of freedom.

CHAPTER 12

THE "HAMMER" WHO WON THE WAR

The moon shone down on the battlefield, casting eerie shadows across the raised plain and among the tall trees. Groans from the wounded and dying disturbed the silence. Injured horses also lay strewn among the fallen, their occasional screams piercing the air. The sounds had grown less frequent as the night wore on, and the men at the top of the rise had grown more restless.

A shadowy figure of a foot soldier approached the prince. "Any word?"

The soldier shook his head. "Nothing, sir."

The prince didn't like it. From the moon's position he could tell it must be near four in the morning; the enemy was certain to have regrouped by now, ready to attack again. What were they waiting for?

"Send another man to check the perimeter!" he ordered. He then sat on the ground, utterly fatigued. The stench of blood and death filled the air, but he didn't notice. His thoughts were drawn to the day's events.

The battle had started early that morning when the Muslim commander Emir Abdul Rahman Al Ghafiqi and his eighty thousand men, among them many horsemen, launched the attack. The prince had known the city of Tours was Al Ghafiqi's next prize, so moving his troops over back roads to avoid being seen, he had positioned them between Al Ghafiqi's army and that city. The high, wooded plain where he made camp forced the enemy's cavalry and troops to charge uphill in order to meet the prince's men.

He mentally congratulated himself on having chosen this location to meet the Muslim troops. The prince had relied on every stratagem he could devise, because he knew his men were outnumbered at least five to one. He remembered how Al Ghafiqi, finding the prince's men at the top of the hill in a large square, had reconsidered. Day after day they had waited for Al Ghafiqi to attack; a week they had waited. This morning the fighting had finally begun.

The prince let out a heavy sigh. The enemy had eventually broken through his troops' lines, attempting to kill him, but his personal guard repulsed the attack, while at another part of the field Al Ghafiqi himself had been killed. That was toward the close of day, and the Muslim army had retreated. It had given the prince time to regather his troops in anticipation of the second attack, for which they were still waiting. Many of their enemy had died, but the prince knew their forces still far outnumbered his own.

"You think they are waiting for us to make a move?" It was his second-in-command who had approached from his side.

The prince grunted and then responded, "Let them wait." After all, he had been waiting for months to meet this fearsome enemy.

Much hinged on the outcome of this battle. Barely a century before, a young orphan boy had had a series of visions. After his first vision he remained silent. Three years passed, and then he was commanded to share the knowledge he had received. He proclaimed himself a prophet of God and began teaching what he had learned. The events that ensued would come to impact the entire world.

That young boy, Mohammed, went on to lead a major religious movement, Islam. As Mohammed's following grew, they gained religious, political, and economic power, eventually controlling all the major commerce routes on land and sea. Not content with controlling the economic routes, Islam and the Saracens united to gain political control of everything from India to Spain. The next in line was France, which should have been an easy target. The combined forces of the Muslims and Saracens had twenty-three years of experience. They were tested on land and on sea. The Frankish army, on the other hand, had much less experience and starkly lesser numbers.

But their leader, Prince Charles, had earned his byname Martel or "the Hammer" for a reason. He was not one to easily give up, particularly when the stakes were high, and for France and all of the western world the stakes had never been higher. Were he to lose, the Muslim troops would likely gain control of the entire western world. He alone, and his little army, stood against their march to victory and the end of western civilization.

When the sun rose, Prince Charles Martel stood at the edge of the rise, looking out over the field below. The enemy was gone. With their commander dead, the Muslim troops had surprisingly continued their retreat all the way to Iberia. He had won.

Later, his family would describe what happened in these words: "Prince Charles drew up his battle lines against the Arabs, and the warrior rushed in against them. With Christ's help he overturned their tents and hastened to battle to grind them small in slaughter. King Abdirama [Al Ghafiqi] having been killed, he destroyed them, driving forth the army, he fought and won. Thus did the victor triumph over his enemies.... Charles scattered them like stubble."

Charles Martel is a founding figure of the underground freedom movement because he carried the torch of freedom forward during the Middle Ages. Had it not been for his leadership, the tide of western civilization would have turned, and the world as we know it today would be drastically different. Also because of his victory at the Battle of Tours, two other key characters were prepared for impact: his friend Saint Boniface became a great evangelizer of Germany, and later on, his grandson Charlemagne became the first Roman emperor in the west in more than three hundred years.

The Hammer, Charles Martel, inspires us today to remember we are not alone in facing great odds. Those wishing to carry on the torch of liberty focus on the importance of their task and what is at stake, rather than the likelihood of victory, and often in doing so, they bring the unimaginable into reality.

LESSONS FROM CHARLES MARTEL ON HOW TO PASS THE TORCH

1. Adversity is a teacher of greatness. Charles Martel learned how to lead and gained courage to face great foes by being thrust into adversity in his personal life and as leader of France. From being imprisoned by his stepmother after his father's death to facing enormous odds on the battle-field, he learned not to fear adversity but to find in it a source of inner strength.

2. Historically, the victors in war are not always those with the biggest troops, the most money, and the greatest experience. What matters most isn't numbers. A great leader inspires people around a shared vision and compelling cause, enabling them to best overwhelming odds.

CHAPTER 13

THE PRECOCIOUS READER WHO BECAME A GREAT KING

"Come, boys! See what I have here!" The boys were in the middle of a good-natured tug-of-war over a toy wooden sword. They pummeled each other, fists clenched tight as the smallest one shouted out, "It's mine! Leave me alone!" The one saying those words was hidden from view as his larger, older brothers piled on top of him, trying to wrest the sword away.

The queen's voice rang out, "Isn't this book beautiful?" Suddenly the sword was relinquished.

The six-year-old little warrior struggled free and ran to his mother's side. "A new book?" His eyes grew bright as he climbed on her lap. "Show me, Mother! Please!" The other boys gathered around with somewhat less interest.

"This," the queen said proudly, "is a book of poetry!" She turned to a page beautifully illustrated with bright colors that seemed to fly off the page. Never before had they seen such a wonderful book. "Listen!" she urged, and began to read.

As the lines of poetry rolled from her tongue, the young boy seemed to drift to another realm. At its end he begged for another poem and then another. After reading a little while longer, she announced, "I have a surprise!"

The boys turned their full attention from the book to her words. "What is it, Mother?" asked the oldest boy, almost as tall as she, though not yet twelve years old. "Are we to have a new riding horse?"

"No," she replied, picking up the book carefully in her arms. "Something else. Something even better! The first of you to learn to read this book shall have it all to yourself!"

Their eyes grew wide. "Teach me right now, Mother!" cried the youngest, and the queen laughed in response.

"I shall not," she answered him, "but each of you may do what you will to learn how to read."

The boy's smile turned to a pout. "But I am only six! Aethelred will certainly learn before me. It's not fair!"

The queen drew her son close. "As he may, but you are just as capable as is he to learn to read." She gently pulled his face close to hers and looked him directly in the eyes. "You may surprise him yet—and yourself. See what you can do if you really want it!" With that she laid the book on the table and left the room.

For the next few days the boys clamored around the book, examining its pictures with delight, fighting over who got to hold it and whose turn it was to turn the pages. Reading proved no easy task, however, and learning to pronounce the strange marks and form the sounds into words took real effort. Each morning the queen read from the book and asked, "Who will be the first to read from this book?"

Each boy would look at the others and shout, "I will!"

One morning the young boy opened the book and turned to a favorite page with a beautiful picture of a young man and his trusty mount. His mother began:

He who thought wisely
on this foundation,
and pondered deeply
on this dark life,
wise in spirit,
remembered often from afar
many conflicts,
and spoke these words:

"Wait, Mother," the young boy interrupted, "it's my turn!" To her astonishment he began to read.

"Where is the horse gone? And where the youth?
Where the giver of the treasure?
Where are the seats at the feast?
Where are the revels in the hall?"[19]

His mother hugged him tightly. "You did it! Alfred, you did it!"

"I found a tutor and learned to read all on my own, Mother!" he explained. He smiled triumphantly. The book was his!

Thus began the education of one of only two English monarchs ever to be given the title "the Great." Alfred's education continued when, still in his youth, he accompanied his father to the Holy Land. There he observed the importance of education, as he found that the church there held an almost complete monopoly on knowledge. The holy texts were only available in Latin, and those who could read that language were few.

Perhaps it was also there that the idea was instilled deep within him that true Christian kingship entails a genuine responsibility toward country and that those entrusted with a crown are given their power by God. This view would be uniquely held by the English monarchs for over a thousand years.

Alfred the Great lived during one of the most dreary and calamitous periods: the medieval times. His country and the surrounding areas were constantly under siege by the Danes. Peace was infrequent and costly. His father, uncles, and brothers all fought against the Danish Vikings, seeking for some measure of peace for their people. When Alfred was appointed monarch, the country was suffering the ravages of constant war. The Vikings mercilessly plundered England's coasts and cities.

Alfred had a plan. He paid a hefty sum to persuade the Vikings to leave his people in peace for a few years. Knowing that kind of peace was much costlier than he could long afford, he took full advantage of the time they were left alone. He called on his Frisian neighbors, able seamen, to help build up the first English navy, creating a force that could rival and even best the Danish fleet. In addition, he reformed the English military with a network of fortresses distributed at strategic points throughout the kingdom. (Later, these well-garrisoned, massive earthen walls were called *burhs* or *boroughs*.) These changes contributed to a lasting defeat of the Vikings on English soil, but Alfred knew his work had only begun.

Next he turned his sights to the lack of education that had permeated his country during its focus on war. His childhood passion for knowledge and literature inspired him to establish a system of general education for all his people. He donated half of his income to the church and schools and attracted scholars from throughout Europe. He encouraged his population to study English, Latin, and the liberal arts.

Winston Churchill said that during Alfred's reign, the nation of England came to birth. Edmund Burke, speaking in admiration of his efforts, wrote, "One cannot help being amazed that a prince who lived in such turbulent times…could have bestowed so much of his time on religious exercises and speculative knowledge."[20]

Alfred the Great truly left an important mark on history. He demonstrated that leadership and moral character are synonymous and that both are benefited by education. Freedom results from valuing and demonstrating each of those things.

LESSONS FROM ALFRED THE GREAT ON HOW TO PASS THE TORCH

1. One certain thing about leadership is that its absence is clearly evident. Problems within a country, community, family, or relationships illustrate where someone has not accepted responsibility and taken leadership. Truly rising to leadership involves learning to solve the problem at hand, as demonstrated by Alfred the Great.

2. Unlike today's politically correct politicians, King Alfred wanted his country to be a Christian nation. He once wrote, "Local government ought to be synonymous with local Christian virtue; otherwise it becomes local tyranny, local corruptions, and local iniquity." Liberty and morality require each other.

CHAPTER 14

THE WEALTHY BEGGAR

"Francesco, come with us to the river! There will be wine, music, dancing—you must come!" The young man who spoke was in high spirits. Though it was early in the day, it seemed he was already drunk.

"Yes," chimed in a young woman, clad in rich garments, "you must join us today. No excuses!"

Francesco smiled. "I promised my father I would sell in the market this morning. I'll join you this afternoon if I finish early."

"Can't one of your brothers or sisters go to the market?" complained the young woman. Francesco only smiled in response as both friends turned and left him to his task of gathering fine silks and velvets into a cart. Though he was missing out on the fun his friends would have, Francesco whistled merrily. His naturally cheery disposition always seemed to win out. Slowly he made his way to the market square.

"Good morning, Francesco!" He was greeted warmly by all he passed, and he smiled and waved in return. It was a busy morning, and soon a short line had formed behind his cart.

"Your father always sells the best goods, Francesco," remarked one customer.

"Yes," the woman next in line replied, "and he charges the most for it too!" Those in line laughed good-naturedly.

"If you weren't satisfied with the quality and prices, Clare, I wouldn't see you nearly every week!" observed Francesco. His response evoked even more laughter from the group. Clare's husband was known to complain about how much his wife spent on the silks and velvets she found in the market. She blushed and began a reply but was interrupted.

"Please, sir, have you anything to give a man in need?" The crowd looked in disdain as a beggar approached the line, though the young merchant's eyes showed concern.

"Go away!" one man called out sharply. "Leave us be! Go beg at the churches if you are unwilling to work like the rest of us!"

"My back—" the beggar began, but he was roughly pushed aside by a man pulling a cart of vegetables through the narrow market streets.

"Out of the way!" yelled the man, and the beggar, bent far over, slowly made his way down the street.

Francesco watched in dismay.

"Don't look so alarmed," said Clare, whose turn it was to purchase her goods. "Those beggars deserve what they have!" she continued, but Francesco didn't hear her words.

He quickly finished selling to those in line and then ran to a nearby merchant. "Pietro, will you watch my cart please? I'll only be a minute!" And in an instant he was running down the street, glancing into every alleyway and corner.

He didn't need to run far. Soon he saw the beggar, sitting in a trash pile. He was digging through the scraps and fending off stray dogs with a broken stick.

Francesco gently touched his arm. "Sir, please, let me help you."

The man's eyes opened wide as the young man emptied one pocket, then another, until he had given him everything he had.

"Thank you, thank you!" the beggar mumbled over and over, as he openly wept.

Just then Francesco noticed his friends watching from across the street. "I thought you went to the river," he called out in mild dismay.

"And we thought you were selling goods—not giving them away!" responded Clare, which set his friends and everyone within earshot laughing. Francesco shook his head as his friends left him alone with the beggar. He helped the man to his feet and brushed the trash from his clothes.

"If you need anything, you know where to find me," he said kindly, and the beggar continued to thank him and slowly went on his way.

When he returned home that evening, his father was furious. "What do you think you're doing, Francesco? I send you to the market to sell, and you come home with empty pockets *and* an empty cart! What kind of fool gives away his wealth? And I thought you had some business sense!"

The young man stood uncomfortably. "The beggar had *nothing*, Father—he was digging through the trash for food! How could I not help?"

Francesco's father was unmoved. "This is the last time I want to hear of this happening, Francesco, the last time!"

"I'm sorry, Father," the young man replied simply. Then he turned and went back outside. It was dark, damp, and cold, and he immediately wished he'd taken a cloak with him. Then he thought again of the beggar who had nothing and reminded himself he should be grateful he had a home to return to.

He wandered along a country path that led along a riverbank and through quiet meadows. He often walked alone here, though not usually at night. The long walks helped still the restlessness within him, and the churches and chapels he found along the way, though in great disrepair, filled him with both a longing and a purpose he found nowhere else.

His father's wealth, he recognized, had given him an easy life. True, when he'd served as a soldier, he'd spent a year in prison as a captive of war, but even then he had food and water, and when he returned home, he'd been given everything he could imagine. He had always lived the same life as his peers, a life of plenty—a life of sin, he called it, and something within him wanted that to change.

The darkness and cold of the night chilled him deeply, but he did not turn home yet. He stood overlooking a small valley and another crumbling church. Something within him called him to more—to what, he did not know. But follow it he must; follow it he did.

Francesco began to avoid the festivals and feasts of his friends. He spent much time alone, often in churches, praying for enlightenment and peace. Not far from his home were the lazar houses, the quarantined homes for the lepers, and he began regularly serving there.

This, in turn, led to a pilgrimage to Rome. There, as he prayed, he had a vision of Jesus Christ. He was told, "Go and repair my house which, as you can see, is falling into ruins." Selling more of his father's cloth, he began to repair the church. His father, again furious at his son's actions, beat him and then sued him. His son returned the money he had taken, along with all the clothes and belongings he had ever received from his father. He then announced he was following a new Father, who would provide all he needed.

From that day forward he was filled with a passion and purpose unlike any he had known before. His heart was filled with the love of God, and he began to preach sermons out of the joy of his heart. The small crowds who listened to him gradually increased, and then came the followers who wanted to live a similar life. He sent them out in pairs at first and then twelve by twelve. The whole countryside came alive with his preaching, and when the pope approved his actions, the order of Franciscans formally came to be. The whole heart of Italy was stirred by this movement, and for the first time since the beginning of the Dark Ages, people's souls began to be awakened.

Francesco, Saint Francis of Assisi, followed his passion and purpose. His efforts served as a precursor to the inspiration of later artists, sculptors, and writers including Giotto, Dante, and Petrarch. The inspiration he provided also contributed to what became known as the Renaissance, a movement that would forever shape the future of the western world.

LESSONS FROM SAINT FRANCIS OF ASSISI ON HOW TO PASS THE TORCH

1. Seeing a society in decay awakened Francis's inner passion to make a difference. Likewise, we all inherit life's circumstances, but they can pave the way for how we respond. Saint Francis could have chosen the easy way and lived the life his father and friends expected of him, but he gave it up in pursuit of a calling that would change the world. He recognized there was something more that God required of him; he sought it out and followed it, regardless of the cost.

2. It often takes time and dedication to discover the path that will bring us our greatest fulfillment and peace. Saint Francis lived as a wealthy son, a soldier, a pilgrim, a merchant, and a beggar. Through years of searching and pondering, he found a path that led to a great transformation for himself and the world around him.

3. Joy is a powerful attractor. Saint Francis of Assisi was at times opposed and wrongly accused, but he allowed the joy within him to dominate, and as a result he saw the good in life and spread it through thought, word, and deed.

PART III

THE RENAISSANCE AND REFORMATION

The Middle Ages usually refers to the time between the fall of the Roman Empire, in the fifth century, and the Renaissance of the Classical Age, around AD 1400. Following the collapse of the Roman Empire, a system called feudalism arose in France and spread throughout Europe.

Here we see the emergence of the second form of the "Power Matrix," as described by best-selling author and leadership expert Orrin Woodward in his book *And Justice for All*. This is where power is shifted from physical control to land control. During this period the vast majority of people lived as peasants under a manorial economy and feudal political system. An important series of events transpired during these centuries.

The "Black Death" struck in 1348, killing one third of Europe's population (an estimated 100-200 million people). Around the same time the Hundred Years' War dominated the French and English regions, stretching from 1317 to 1453. As a result of the drawn-out war, manorial governments burdened the poor classes with massive war debt. The economic situation was worsened as governments manipulated currencies to attempt to pay their debts. This caused the little money people had to further lose its value. Prices rose and economic health plummeted.

The Italian scholar Petrarch (circa 1341) recognized in this time a dearth of knowledge and liberty, as compared to the ages that came before it. He wrote of it: "My fate is to live amid varied and confusing storms. But for you perhaps, if as I hope and wish you will live long after me, there will follow a better age. This sleep of forgetfulness will not last forever. When the darkness has been dispersed, our descendants can come again in the former pure radiance."[21]

The darkness Petrarch spoke of referred to the dearth of classical ideas and literature and the absence of the flame of liberty. Reason and truth, which had once been commonplace and "radiant," were gone. In speaking of darkness, he also referred to a strict reliance on faith alone and an insistence that people rely on the Church for direction and truth.

Today we may think our circumstances differ vastly from the darkness of the Middle Ages. It is true we have witnessed, and continue to witness, an outpouring of new inventions. It's also true that the desire for freedom continues to spread throughout the world.

However, we have in common with Petrarch's time a severe dearth of knowledge surrounding the source of our liberties. We too live in a time of darkness where people do not know what came before them and do not appreciate the sacrifices that won them the fading liberty they enjoy. While we have access to knowledge like never before, our challenge is to seek it out; our duty is to pay the price to learn what it takes to be free and to learn the history of all that preceded us, to ensure future generations their freedom.

By the advent of the printing press, about a hundred years after Petrarch, people's minds were prepared for a renaissance of literature and Greek and Roman ideas. They were anxious to return to the past lessons of history. As books became more widely available, the everyday man and woman had unprecedented access to ideas and lessons from the past.

What followed changed the world in an unknown magnitude. Peasants revolted, believing they deserved a better future. Monarchic theocracy was threatened as Bible reading became commonplace and religion became a more individual matter. New ideas spread like wildfire—the idea that humans were not meant to be divided and pitted against one another but that they were created to be free; that people could read and reason for themselves; and that they needed no distant inter-preter to understand God's word.

During the Renaissance the flame of liberty leapt forth and flew across the globe, one person here, another there, until Europe was dotted with men and women hungry for truth and willing to sacrifice on its behalf, stepping toward liberty, torches carried high. Will we follow in their steps?

CHAPTER 15

CICERO'S APPRENTICE

"Hello, son."

The young man was shocked to see his father standing at the door. "Hello—come in!" His mind began to race. *Why is my father here? Did something happen back home?*

His father did not speak but surveyed the small room in silence. "Is everything all right, Father?"

"That is what I have come here to see, son. Are you enjoying Bologna?"

The son cleared his throat. In truth he was enjoying the city but not for the reasons his father would have hoped. He had been sent here to study law. That was, after all, the same path his father had pursued, and he knew how much his father desired him to follow in his shoes. "I am enjoying the city, Father…." What more could he say?

"Good," his father replied as he began to examine the room. "How is school?" He lifted some papers on the boy's desk and grunted. "Cicero?" he asked with arched eyebrows. The son's eyes shifted to his bed, then back to his father. His father began to walk toward the bed, and the young man silently cursed himself. *Not under the bed, Father, not under the bed!*

"School, Father!" he called out, attempting to redirect his father's attention, crossing to the desk and shuffling the papers loudly. "School is moving along!"

His father knelt and pulled up the bedcover, and the young man cried out, "Father! Please!"

"What is this?" his father asked, each word tinged with anger. "Cato? Tacitus? Livy?" His voice rose with every name, and he threw one work after the other onto the floor of the room. "Juvenal? Varro? Aeschylus?"

"Father, please calm down!"

Heedlessly his father continued, his face red with fury. "Aristotle? Homer? Plutarch!" With the final name he grabbed an armful of books, and then threw the pile angrily into the fire that was warming the room.

"No! No! Father!" The young man knelt by the flames as his father continued to throw one book after another into the fire.

"I sent you here to study law! And what do I find? You waste my money and my time by reading these books?" His father continued piling the books into the fire until the makeshift bookcase was empty. Only then did he notice his son, trembling uncontrollably, sobs shaking his body.

"Father, I didn't intend to disappoint you! But my books! My books!"

Suddenly touched by his son's grief he pulled two works from the leaping flames, a Cicero and a Virgil. He threw them at his son's feet. "If you must study Latin," he said with disgust and resignation, "at least make time for some law as well. Don't waste your time or my money." With that he turned and left the room.

Francesco Petrarca, or Petrarch, spent seven years studying law at his father's behest, but he considered the entire study a waste. He much preferred reading and writing, and to his credit he found much success doing both. His first work, *Africa*, which detailed the life of Roman general Scipio Africanus, contributed to his becoming a celebrity of sorts in Europe. Later he would be crowned by a Roman senator the first poet laureate since antiquity.

Petrarch's status allowed him the unusual privilege of traveling for pleasure, and everywhere he traveled, he would stop at monasteries in search of books he had never before seen. It was in this manner that he one day discovered a collection of letters written by Cicero that had been lost to time, and ever after he considered this his greatest find.

His love for Cicero's writing was immense. He greatly disdained the morals and attitudes of his own time and found in Cicero a champion of liberty and morality who refreshed and enlivened him. He relished Cicero's words and works and combined the knowledge he gained from Cicero with the spiritual wisdom he found in Augustine. He held in contempt the current academic system, writing, "I dwelt especially upon antiquity, for our own age has always repelled me."

Petrarch's wide travels and tireless efforts seeking out the ancient classics set in motion a revival of ancient texts that would in turn spark the Renaissance. He wrote profusely, and his works restored the recognition of literature. The old ideas he uncovered and new ideas thus generated propelled people to action and caused many to emerge from an educational darkness.

Petrarch is said to have been the first to restore the values society had lost during the Dark Ages. Because of the renaissance of ideas and literature kindled by Petrarch, feudalism and the manorial economic system that had held people in captivity since the Dark Ages began to erode. Art and music were affected, and both began to flourish. Commerce expanded, and the cloth, silk, and wool markets exploded. Venice became a center for printing, and the republican form of government was reinstituted there.

Petrarch's unquenchable appetite for knowledge led to his study of Euclid, Ptolemy, Galen, Livy, Virgil, Plato, Aristotle, and others. He found in these philosophers and their writings an embodiment of Christian virtues. His focus on the achievement of individual potential led to a renewed interest in the moral and political values of society.

The more he read, the more he realized the depraved conditions around him were not how humanity was meant to live. He believed that people were designed to be happy and to prosper. "Happiness," he wrote, "is small and hidden and must be dug out by a more thorough investigation…. As I select the best from the many [classical works], are these a small cause of joy to you; the image and similitude of God the Creator within the human soul, the mind, memory, providence, eloquence?"

Petrarch's thirst for knowledge and tireless efforts to find and study ancient classics produced a period of spiritual renewal. That renewal then paved the way for those who followed to understand and appreciate the importance of liberty and morality and underscored the importance of education in preserving both of them.

LESSONS FROM PETRARCH ON HOW TO PASS THE TORCH

1. Petrarch's time, like our own, was riddled with problems. Writes Stanford professor Louis W. Spitz of that time, "Government was burdened from war debts, indulged in monetary manipulation, devalued the currency and debasement [sic] of coinage. Taxes became increasingly more oppressive."[22] Barbarian invasions following the fall of Rome resulted in a loss of the knowledge and liberty that had sprung from the Roman Republic. Refugees, often with manuscripts, streamed west, and these are the works Petrarch sought out and found. Similarly, we must find and study classical works that illuminate lessons from history and demonstrate what we must do today to defend liberty and morality.

2. Petrarch's appreciation of the classics triggered a revolutionary development of European culture that led into the Renaissance. It's not enough for us alone to study these classic works; our passion for their truths must propel us to help make their knowledge more widely known and appreciated.

CHAPTER 16

THE MORNING STAR WITH THE SILVER TONGUE

*Session One: 4 May 1415, Cathedral of
Constance, Council of Constance*

66 "Holy brethren, of the most holy synod of Constance!"
The priest's voice rang through the halls of the church.
For six months the priests had gathered to deliberate
matters of importance to the Catholic Church, and today's meeting held a topic of interest to everyone in attendance. "We are assembled today in the Holy Spirit, for the purpose of eradicating errors and heresies which are sprouting beneath its shade."

Heads nodded in assent. Just recently Jerome of Prague and
John Hus had arrived in Rome, both guilty of heresy. Every day a
new heretic seemed to arise! The priest continued: "We learn that
the Catholic faith has been attacked by false followers, desirous of
the world's glory. They are led by proud curiosity to know more
than they should. In our times, their leader and prince was that
pseudo-Christian John Wycliffe!"

Shouts of anger arose in the crowd. When they had quieted, the
speaker resumed. "Many scandals, losses, and dangers to the souls

have resulted from his writings and errors. This holy synod repudiates and condemns forever by this decree all of John Wycliffe's works. It is forbidden they should be read, taught from, expounded, or cited for any reason whatsoever. It forbids each and every Catholic henceforth, under pain of anathema, to preach, teach, or affirm in public the said articles or books, treatises, volumes, and pamphlets, which are to be burnt in public."

Cheers arose, but the priest was not through with his condemnation.

"Furthermore!" His voice rose in volume and eloquence. "This holy synod declares, defines, and decrees that the said John Wycliffe died a heretic, and it anathematizes him and condemns his memory. It decrees and orders that his body and bones are to be exhumed, if they can be identified among the corpses of the faithful, and to be scattered far from the burial place of the church!"[23]

Though Wycliffe had been dead thirty years, the Roman Catholic authorities followed through on their decree. Fuller described the results of this action: "They burnt his bones to ashes and cast them into Swift, a neighboring brook running hard by. Thus this brook hath conveyed his ashes into Avon, Avon into Severn, Severn into the narrow seas, they into the main ocean. And thus the ashes of Wycliffe are the emblem of his doctrine, which now is dispersed the world over."[24]

John Foxe, of *Foxe's Book of Martyrs*, describes it this way: "[T]hough they digged up his body, burnt his bones and drowned his ashes, yet the Word of God and the truth of his doctrine, with the fruit and success thereof, they could not burn; which yet to this day...doth remain."[25]

John Wycliffe was born in the mid-1320s in Yorkshire, England, to a well-to-do family. His life was influenced by key historic events, including the Black Death in his twenties, when one third to one half of Europe's population was lost. Throughout his life he frequently referred to this event and the darkness that prevailed during that period.

The Hundred Years' War between France and England also raged during his lifetime, changing many political, religious, and economic aspects of life. Wage controls locked the poor of the time into a menial existence, and papal authority held tight control over the secular powers of the day. This resulted in a violent Peasants' Revolt, triggered by a new tax levy. Though Wycliffe was one of the most educated men of his time, he was well aware that those around him were plagued by illiteracy and economic bondage.

In his later years, Wycliffe served as a professor of theology at Oxford; he also held a doctorate in theology. That degree and position enabled him to read and speak about religious texts that few others were allowed to study. The study of the Bible was closely regulated, and no one was allowed to translate it without a bishop's license, meaning that ordinary people, who rarely read at all and never read or spoke Latin, the language of the Bible, had virtually no direct access to the sacred work.

Wycliffe was bothered by this circumstance and determined to do something about it. His actions were destined to be noticed, for he was no quiet disturber. He was known to have a brilliant mind, undaunted courage, and what some have called "a silver tongue."

The Bible truths, Wycliffe knew, would inspire the common people with a faith and courage that could break the economic and political bondage and oppression he saw everywhere around him.

He determined, with the help of some close friends and scholars, to translate the Bible and create new copies of the Bible, all by hand.

Though he died before his work was entirely complete, and though the Catholic Church sought out those Bibles and each of his writings and burned and condemned them, copies of his Bibles continued to be found and influence people for more than a century after his death, until printed Bibles took their place. Wycliffe's Bible would, in time, greatly influence William Tyndale, who made the first printed translation of the New Testament into English.

In life and in death Wycliffe inspired followers. Wrote William Thorpe, "I indeed clove to none closer than to him, the wisest and most blessed of all men whom I have ever found. From him one could learn in truth what the church of Christ is and how it should be ruled and led."

John Hus, his follower who was later condemned to die at the stake by the same council that exhumed Wycliffe's bones and burned them, wished that his "soul might be wherever that of Wycliffe was found."

Wycliffe, the "morning star of the Reformation," serves as an important reminder that those who stand for truth must expect resistance and even oppression, sometimes even after their death. But those willing to withstand that opposition, as Wycliffe did, often have impact that bends the course of history and paves the way for greater happiness and liberty.

LESSONS FROM WYCLIFFE ON HOW TO PASS THE TORCH

1. Wycliffe spoke his mind about the truths he found and was not popular among those who had the power of oppression. However, his honesty gave him great sway among those who recognized the truth of his words. Standing for truth is often unpopular and sometimes politically incorrect. It requires conviction to take such a stand and be willing to persevere, even when those in power seek to thwart one's cause.

2. Wycliffe might be seen as an extremist set against today's relativistic culture, but his courage and conviction were what allowed him to move the dial of liberty away from greater bondage toward greater freedom. "Extremism" has its place in a relativistic society. His handwritten copies of the Bible, considered sacrilege at the time, were the first real step toward widespread biblical literacy, commencing when Bibles were first spread hand to hand.

CHAPTER 17

THE SECRET THAT CHANGED THE WORLD

"Johann!" Someone rapped angrily on the door. "Johann! I know you're in there! Open up!"

Johann sat in darkness, not responding, hoping to be left alone. He did not wish to speak to Mr. Fust. When the man finally left his doorstep, he breathed a sigh of relief. He waited in silence and darkness for a long time, and only when he was certain Johann Fust had left for good did he relight the single candle sitting on the table next to him.

His heart beat more rapidly as he carefully uncovered the book of Psalms. *His* book of Psalms. Yes, he thought to himself, he could call it that. Though tomorrow it would be gone with nearly everything else in the room, today it was still his.

His hands trembled as he gently turned the pages. *He had created this!* Though he no longer owned the press or the manuscripts or even this book—the idea had been *his*. Could Johann Fust ever have conceived of the two type sizes that characterized the Psalter? Could his colleague and confidant, Guttenberg's own former apprentice, Peter Schoeffer, ever have imagined the three-color print that brought the Psalter to life? No, neither Fust nor Schoeffer could have created this. He knew that much. It had been his idea and his inspiration that had conceived the whole work.

Ten years ago it had begun, when inspiration struck. Books were traditionally handwritten, or printed one page at a time, each page painstakingly carved, word by word, out of one block of wood. It was highly inefficient and costly. Johann had long grappled with the question of how to improve the process.

He still remembered the moment when as a thunderbolt a picture lit his mind: a picture of a single letter. Instantly he had asked himself, "Why carve out an entire page that can be used for printing only one page of one book? Why not carve out single letters that can be used and reused, moved and adjusted, to create an infinite combination of words, pages, and books?"

The inventor within him had been driven to try it out at once, developing an early prototype, and the perfectionist within him propelled him to try one thing after another, in pursuit of the most durable, precise, and aesthetic movable-type printing press. And he had done it. Despite setback after setback, he had done it. But at what cost! His heart was full of grief at what had happened. For almost ten years, he had managed to keep his invention a secret from the public, but his greatest opportunity was also his greatest mistake. He could see that now.

"Fust and Schoeffer," that's what the Psaltery read. Schoeffer, the young man who had so cunningly entered his tutelage as an apprentice, whom he had so carefully trained in the art of movable print. And Johann Fust, his supposed benefactor, who provided the essential funds needed for the final push to print the Bible! Who so generously provided loans, twice provided them, and promised no interest. It was too good to be true.

Yes, the Bible had been published—but by whom? Fust, in a bitter twist of fate, sued Gutenberg for unpaid loans *and* interest. Schoeffer, the unassuming apprentice, had testified against him in court, and he had lost. He had lost his press; he had lost his Bibles. He had lost all, it seemed. He wondered bitterly whether they had been in collusion from the start. In the morning they would come and take it all away, and he would have to begin all over again.

What had he written his friend, when the secret about his printing press was first out? "It is a press, certainly, but a press from which shall soon flow inexhaustible streams of the most abundant and most marvelous liquor that has flowed to relieve the thirst of man! Through it God will spread His Word. A spring of pure truth shall flow from it! Like a new star, it shall scatter the darkness of ignorance, and cause a light heretofore unknown to shine among men."

That, at least, was some consolation for him. Even if he were forgotten, even if the Bibles and manuscripts, the Psalters and letters could not be traced to his name, at least they could be traced. At least they existed! The thought gave him courage. Though he was heartbroken, he could rest in the knowledge that he, Johann Gutenberg, had done something to change the world.

Little is known about Johann Gutenberg. Most of what we do know about his life is from legal records and historical events: an uprising in his youth, leading to his first experience as a refugee of sorts; that he mentored a wealthy tradesman in polishing gems; and there is record of a broken promise of marriage to a woman from Strasbourg.

We know he loved to read and that the lack of books led him to search for a way to duplicate them more efficiently. Before Gutenberg, few could afford a book of their own. Libraries were limited to monasteries and churches. But the printing press, with movable type, changed everything. His invention took civilization from a place of darkness into the most intellectually and artistically enlightened period in the history of the world.

His genius helped the masses gain literacy. It caused knowledge and advanced modern science and literature to spread more quickly than ever before. His invention essentially launched the Middle Ages full throttle into the Renaissance and Reformation period; without it, the two periods would most certainly not have occurred.

Soon after Gutenberg's invention, presses sprang up all over the world, from Denmark to Hungary, from Spain to Poland. This profusion of printed material and knowledge altered the structure of society dramatically. It allowed for mass communication and virtually unrestricted information. Revolutionary ideas transcended borders, time, and space and threatened those in power. Almost overnight it conquered the monopoly of education by the literate elite, placing knowledge in the hands of the middle class.

An unimpeded flow of truth followed the invention of the printing press, and thanks in large part to Johann Gutenberg, the body politic moved from bondage to revolt to liberty.

LESSONS FROM GUTENBERG ON HOW TO PASS THE TORCH

1. When information flows freely, freedom and education result. Third-world countries currently demonstrate this shift from bondage to freedom and religious liberty. South Korea boasts one of the fastest growing economies, as well as five of the world's biggest churches. Religious liberties in China today are also continuing to expand. Some statistics have China at one hundred million Christians. Christians grew in Africa from 9 percent at the turn of the twentieth century to 44 percent today.

2. On the other hand, the West now lies on the other side of the body politic, leaning on the edge of apathy toward bondage. Reading and literacy is at an all time low as we take our hard earned freedoms for granted. Widespread education is required to maintain a middle class, and as education spirals downward, the middle class is disappearing in the West. Freedom, morality and prosperity suffer as a result.

CHAPTER 18

THE SCHOLAR-PRINCE OF PORTUGAL

66 "Tell me the story again, Mama!" the young child pled.

"Again?" said the queen. "Why, I've already told it to you twice. You must go to bed now."

The young boy's eyes filled with tears. "Just once more, *please*, Mama!"

His mother smiled. She certainly had an adventurer in this son. "Perhaps once more—but you must promise to go right to sleep afterwards!"

"I will, I will! I promise!"

She laughed and began her tale: "Far beyond Persia, hidden deep in the Orient, there once lived a Christian king named—"

"Prester John!" the boy interrupted with a shout.

"Shhhh!" his mother whispered. "You'll wake your brother!"

"Sorry," the boy mumbled.

"Prester John," the queen continued. "Long, long ago, his great-great-great-great-grandfather was among the Magi to visit the Lord Jesus Christ. Prester John ruled over seventy kings and was said to have greater riches and power than any other kingdom!" The boy's face lit with a broad smile, imagining his mother's words.

"His land reached from the Tower of Babel to the place where the sun rises and was full majestic buildings, beautiful streets, and well-cared-for homes. In its walls could be found all kinds of great treasure and wealth, and because his kingdom was hidden, no enemy ever threatened its peace or prosperity. His people were kind and generous, and though they lived in peace, they were mighty warriors, cunning with the sword and the bow and arrow.

"Now it happened that far away from Prester John's kingdom the Holy Land was under siege by the Turks, Muslim believers who wished to have the land for themselves. Great battles ensued, and the Christians in Jerusalem were every day threatened by the Turkish armies drawing nearer and nearer. If aid did not arrive soon, all the Christians in the Holy Land would be killed!"

The boy' was wide-eyed, as if hearing the story for the first time.

"That is when the letter arrived!"

"Yes, Mama! Tell me about the letter!" His face shone; this was his favorite part of the story.

"The letter was sent to the emperor, and it was from Prester John. 'We have determined,' said the letter, 'to visit the holy sepulcher of our Lord in Jerusalem with a very large army, in accordance with the glory of our majesty, to humble and chastise the enemies of the Christians.' The letter promised to come to the Christians' aid. But the great Tigris River stood between Prester John and Jerusalem, and Prester John never arrived. Though many have searched for him and his great kingdom, they never have been found."[26]

"I will find them, Mama!" he said, as always, when she finished her story.

She kissed him on the forehead, then stood to leave. "Sleep! You promised!"

"Yes, Mama, I promise." As she left the room, she could hear him repeating the story to himself, word for word.

That young adventurer, Infante Henrique of Portugal, Duke of Viseu, more commonly known as Prince Henry the Navigator, grew into one of the greatest discoverers of all time. His efforts and interests would usher in the Age of Discovery and would beckon fellow adventurers from around the world to his doorstep.

Prince Henry began his adult adventures around the age of twenty, when he first glimpsed the treasures that lay beyond the safe ports of his home, Portugal. He and his brothers and father traveled to the Moorish port of Cueta in Morocco. There they successfully captured the port from Barbary pirates, who had long raided the Portuguese ports and wreaked havoc on Portuguese ships. The pirates called the Port of Cueta home, and so with its successful capture, Henry, his father, and his brothers successfully secured their home ports and shorelines.

But Henry was not content with that first success. The new sights and sounds, the foreign languages and customs, all fascinated him and compelled him to travel further. He began exploring the coast of Africa, which was largely unknown and untraveled by Europeans. To his dismay he found that the ships available to him were too large and heavy to travel the shallow waters and rivers he wished to navigate.

This launched Henry's next initiative—to build a ship capable of sailing *into* the wind and light enough to navigate easily where larger, bulkier ships could not go. The caravel was the result, a light, speedy vessel that proved extremely maneuverable and perfectly fit his exploratory purposes.

Henry's childhood aspirations grew. He envisioned a stop to the slave trade and the spread of Christianity. He foresaw an immense increase in commercial trade and a naval school that would train the best and brightest naval explorers of the day. The possibilities, he felt, were nearly limitless.

True to his vision, Henry established naval trade on an unprecedented scale. He shipped common goods such as salt, wheat, and rice; he shipped spices including cinnamon, peppers, nutmeg, and ginger. He expanded his trade to include rarities from the Orient: magnificent tapestries and carpets that only the wealthiest individuals and traders could afford.

Henry had a genius for systems and an unbounded imagination. Using both, he established the most extensive naval school of the millennium. He trained sailors in geography, navigation, cartography, and research, making them expert in the use of compass and sextant. He built ships for trade, for exploration, for pleasure. His school and endeavors attracted Muslims, Jews, Arabs, Italians, Germans, and Scandinavians. His students were armed not only with knowledge but also with a passion to make a difference and with a penchant for adventure and life on the edge.

The groundbreaking techniques taught in Henry's school allowed for trade and travel paths that had never before been traced. The sailing techniques and shipping styles he developed were later used by Columbus and other great explorers, resulting in the discovery of many previously unknown and unsettled islands, inlets, and sailing routes.

The torch of freedom hinges on political, economic, and religious events and leaders. Prince Henry the Navigator carried the torch by educating a new generation of leaders and developing new systems of navigation that launched a crucial period of exploration and discovery.

LESSONS FROM PRINCE HENRY THE NAVIGATOR ON HOW TO PASS THE TORCH

1. When developing communities of leaders, it is important to have a system in place to support that development. Without the funding and resources provided by his father and brothers as rulers of Portugal, the school Prince Henry developed would never have come about. And without the formal school and resources that he established and developed, the generations of leaders and adventurers and their resultant discoveries would never have happened.

2. Stories and beliefs play a powerful role in shaping history and discoveries. Though the story of Prester John was based in legend, that story inspired Prince Henry toward discoveries and accomplishments that had real impact on future generations. It's worth finding stories that inspire youth and adults alike and using those stories to build character and guide future goals, ensuring that the flame of liberty will continue burning brightly.

CHAPTER 19

THE RUNAWAY SAINT

"**M**y honored father…." The young man's hands trembled as he began the letter. He set his pen down, fearing he would spoil the paper. He knew that when his father read the letter, he would likely be distraught, perhaps even furious. And what would his grandfather, his mentor, think?

Then there was his mother. His heart dropped. If he weren't so sure of his decision, the thoughts of his family would surely have swayed him.

Even now his body was wracked with grief at the path that lay ahead of him. He would be leaving in secret at the break of dawn, without a word about where he was going and without saying good-bye. It would hurt them all deeply. He would leave his letter with his books, in the windowsill where he knew his father would see it, and he would be gone.

The thoughts of what his father and mother would think and feel upon his departure were simply unbearable, and he pushed all such considerations aside. He mustn't dwell on that, not now, not when so much hinged on the decision he had already made.

With a new determination, he took up the pen again. "I doubt not at all that my departure hath been to you painful and distressing…yet I would that by this letter my mind and intention may be fully revealed to thee, that thou may be of a better courage, and may understand that I was led unto the purpose in question by no means in that light and childish spirit as I hear is believed by many persons."

He had heard the rumors that his decision to join the brotherhood of friars was an impetuous, impulsive reaction, a phase he would soon pass through, and that he ought not to follow through with it. But nothing could be further from the truth. He had witnessed "boundless misery" among his fellow men, a fruit of "extreme unrighteousness…adulteries, thefts, idolatries, impurities…blasphemies." Could he find among them any that did good? No, he had decided, he could not.

He continued to write to his father, explaining his decision. "I saw every virtue downtrodden and crushed, and crime and vice promoted and everywhere supreme. Daily did I pray more fervently, 'show thou me, Lord, the way that I should walk in.'" And at last he had found it. The Lord had answered his prayer. He was to leave his home, his family, and his fortune for a life of asceticism, a life with God. He would rather die a thousand deaths than be guilty of abandoning the path that was now so clear. He must do as the Lord had revealed to him.

He finished his letter in a rush of emotion. "Most beloved father, 'let thine eyes cease from tears,' and do not henceforth lament and grieve even more than I do, over myself. I would beg and pray of thee that thou as a man of courage and great heart wouldest do thine utmost to console and strengthen my mother. I constantly pray unto the Lord for the salvation and well-being of your souls. Your son, Girolamo."[27]

He awoke with a start. It was time to go! Courage filled him. Though the thought of leaving everything behind was heart-breaking, the dream he'd been given last night was enough to convince him this was the right path. A shower of ice-cold water had poured over him in his dream, burning away the temptations and troubles that had so long plagued him, leaving him feeling whole and pure. He was prepared to leave all behind for this—for God.

Thus began the lifelong quest of Girolamo Savonarola, a quest for the higher path and purer purpose, a life dedicated to restoring religious reform and republican values to the great city of Florence.

The Florence of Savonarola's day was just entering a golden age of artistic and literary greatness. At the heart of almost all that occurred was the wealthy Medici family, whose influence stretched from banking to textiles to trade and even religion. Savonarola disdained all things Medici and what they represented, including inequality, monarchy, corruption, infidelity—the list went on and on. Lorenzo the Magnificent ruled the house of Medici during the heart of the Renaissance, and it was against him that Savonarola directed some of his most vicious attacks.

As an early Dominican friar, Savonarola had little impact, but when he was transferred to Florence, his influence began to grow, and people began to listen to his critiques and prophecies. Thanks to his having read Dante, Plato, and others and having studied philosophy, logic, and medicine, his speeches were well-grounded and deeply reasoned.

Savonarola was shocked by the worldliness of Florence and dismayed at the violence and insecurity that wracked the city. The people, he observed, were becoming weary of political responsibility. They wished to turn all power over to the Medicis, who had begun to rule more and more despotically. The speeches he shared in response to his observations shocked many but inspired others.

Slowly Savonarola built up a following, and his reputation grew until he was the most famous and influential preacher in the city. In a quick succession of events, Lorenzo de' Medici passed away, succeeded by his son Pietro. King Charles of France, seeing the chaotic circumstances in which Florence was steeped, took advantage of the situation and swept through the Alps with thirty thousand men, rushing in to conquer the city.

Savonarola's dire accusations against the Medicis and astute prophecies about their downfall were now fresh on the minds of the Florentines. He had prophesied a conqueror from the north would arrive, and it seemed that King Charles had fulfilled the prophecy.

Power quickly shifted away from the Medicis and toward Savonarola as a result. The people revolted against Medici power, while Savonarola's followers gained political control as he helped negotiate a peaceful exit by King Charles and his troops. With Pietro de' Medici exiled and King Charles sent on his way, Savonarola and his friends set up a new government, ushering in what he called an era of universal peace. Enlisting the help of the youth of the city to act as citizen-police of sorts, Savonarola began his reforms with strict enforcement of morals throughout Florence.

His power and popularity, however, were short-lived. The pope was not pleased with Savonarola's actions, and within three years

Savonarola was formally excommunicated from the church, exiled, and eventually hanged. His body was burned and his ashes scattered in a nearby river.

What was Savonarola's influence? Author Paul Sristeller writes, "Effective preachers made a deep impact all over fifteenth-century Italy, and sometimes led to revivalist movements and political repercussions of which Savonarola is the most famous.... In Italy no less than in the rest of Europe, the religious guilds directed the activities of the laity and exercised a tremendous influence upon the visual arts, music, and literature."

The Italian Renaissance was shaped significantly by Savonarola, and artists such as Michelangelo, Leonardo, and Raphael, along with thinkers like Machiavelli, in turn were touched to varying degrees by the ideas that Savonarola advocated and spread.

Aspiring torchbearers can learn much from people like Savonarola, who shaped culture and history through their dedicated efforts and single-minded focus.

LESSONS FROM SAVONAROLA ON HOW TO PASS THE TORCH

1. Italy in the fourteenth and fifteenth centuries represents one of the most fascinating episodes of the world's civilization. It is also surprisingly similar to our own time. Elements of adventure, scandal, political corruption, intrigue, and mystery dominate during this period. Studying this important time provides insight about the past that every lover of liberty today should know and understand well.

2. During the Renaissance several breakthroughs occurred that shaped the information age of our world. This period demonstrates that valuable knowledge leads to growth if remembered and acted upon, but if ignored it leads to decline. For us to prosper today we must understand the factors that contribute to freedom and morality and help to promulgate those in our own society today.

CHAPTER 20

A SERIOUS FIGHT OVER SAUSAGE

"Are you ready?" A woman's voice broke the morning stillness, and at the sound of it the man at the window smiled.

"It's beautiful, isn't it?" he replied, looking out at the scene below. The woman joined his side, and together they looked out on the Rhine, a light snow bathing the wide, silent river in wonder.

"It is," she replied. "I never tire of it."

"Nor do I," he agreed, then continued, "I suppose I am ready, though I never feel quite up to the task when I am defending my flock." He looked down toward his desk and picked up a book. It was a well-worn copy of the New Testament, translated and published a few years before by Erasmus.

He opened to Matthew and read aloud, "For where two or three are gathered together in my name, there am I in the midst of them."

He turned to his wife. "Today we gather together for Christ's sake; will He not be with us?"

His wife smiled, "Yes, I believe He will. Though this is no church meeting."

The man laughed softly, then shook his head, "No, it is not. But shall not it determine the content of many future church meetings?"

"Indeed, it shall," the woman responded.

"And perhaps after today's meeting"—he drew in a deep breath and let it out slowly before continuing—"I will marry you, Anna Reinhard!"

She blushed and laughed. "But we are already married!"

He smiled broadly. "You know that, and I know that," his voice grew hushed, "and God knows that. But the city council has yet to condone the marriage of a priest such as I with a woman such as you." He paused. "But one day, Anna, I will marry you, before the council, and before all the people of Zurich. And we shall eat sausage!"

They laughed, and as the man drew her close, he thought about the purpose of his appearance before the Zurich city council that day. It was, indeed, partly because of sausage and partly because of marriage that he was to appear before them, but mostly it was because of his flock. He felt heavily the weight of his calling. That's what had led him in the first place to study Erasmus and to study the Bible.

Most of his colleagues, though priests, had read little of the Bible. But he felt sure the Bible was second only to Christ, and those he led could only know the truth by turning to the words of Christ as contained in the Bible. All of the rules and indulgences with no biblical root had nothing to do with Christ and ought to be expunged. He'd begun preaching directly from the Bible, reading chapters at a time from the pulpit, and within the year his friend, Christoph, had acted in accordance with his preaching.

Christoph Froschauer, a well-known printer, had invited his employees and friends to a dinner during Lent and had at that meal served sausage. According to Catholic doctrine, eating meat during Lent was forbidden. But according to Zwingli and his supporters, that same doctrine was not biblical. Zwingli had defended Christopher against the city council, who had thrown his friend into prison.

"Christians are free to fast or not to fast, because the Bible does not prohibit the eating of meat during Lent!" Zwingli had insisted. A neighboring bishop had sharply criticized him, but the reformer responded by writing sixty-seven theses in the spirit of Luther's Ninety-Five Theses. He had published them before today's hearing and planned to defend them.

It was rumored that his theses were even more eloquent and soundly reasoned than Luther's, but he cared little for the rumors of the day. What mattered to him was that people listened to his message: that the Bible, alone, contained God's word, and people ought to follow what the Bible taught.

Later that day Ulrich Zwingli, the renegade priest, presented himself to the Zurich city council in what came to be known as the First Disputation. "I am ready to be instructed and corrected," he announced plainly, "but only from scripture." Zwingli's persuasive reasoning and deep knowledge of the scriptures that day convinced the city council it was time for change.

The priest, who had survived the Black Death and the wrath of Catholic authorities, did, indeed, publicly marry Anna Reinhard the next year, and his biblical views continued to spread throughout Switzerland and beyond. Under his influence, the strict rules that governed fasting were lifted, images were removed from places of worship, and clerical marriage was approved. His sermons on salvation by faith alone, rather than works, ultimately led to his complete rejection by papal authority.

Under his influence the Swiss Reformation quickly advanced. But the changes he advocated were met with increasing opposition, particularly when his positions were viewed as attacking the political papal authority. Eventually war erupted. It was during the Second Battle of Kapel that Zwingli died. Outnumbered five to one, Zwingli led two thousand men into battle. At its close five hundred reformers were dead, including Zwingli and twenty-four other priests.

Zwingli's life demonstrated that of a true follower of Christ, and he embodied his own words when he described what it really means to follow Christ. "A true Christian is not one who speaks about the laws of God but one who with God's help attempts great things." Zwingli not only attempted great things, he did them. He stood up to the powers of tyranny, standing against corruption and ignorance, encouraging freedom and virtue and thereby moving forward liberty's cause.

LESSONS FROM ULRICH ZWINGLI ON HOW TO PASS THE TORCH

1. Although Zwingli was inspired in part by Martin Luther's words and actions, both men had unique roles to play and powerfully influenced the reform movements in their own countries while doing so in unique ways. Strong leaders with distinct opinions don't always get along, but that shouldn't lessen our respect for them or diminish what we can learn from them.

2. Zwingli's views were highly unpopular among those in authority, and he risked his livelihood and his life defending what he believed to be true. Liberty requires such conviction and determination; without it, liberty's flame falters and then expires.

3. Zwingli insisted he was not an innovator—from his perspective he was simply defending the truth, as found in the pure teachings of the scriptures. This single-minded focus permeated his influence and his life and is another characteristic of those who bear the torch of freedom.

PART IV

THE ENLIGHTENMENT

The Renaissance, beginning in the fourteenth century, ushered in a new era, impacting everything from art, to politics, to religion and beyond. The movement began in Italy and spread throughout Western Europe. Classical ideas and discoveries, once lost, were revisited with a new enthusiasm. Influential thinkers, artists, and leaders arose, including Petrarch, Leonardo da Vinci, Dante Alighieri, Michelangelo, and Niccolò Machiavelli.

Many of these thinkers contributed important fuel to the flame of freedom by reviving the discussion about humanity, their purpose, and their relation to the Creator. In an early way, they also began to discuss the role of government and the need for monarchs' power to be limited, at least to some extent.

During this time an idea called humanism arose. Humanism encouraged all to study the "humanities," or topics including history, moral philosophy, rhetoric, and poetry. Through the study of these matters, humanists believed, men and women would be best prepared to participate in their local communities and governments and be enabled to communicate with clarity and depth of thought.

One author wrote of the movement, "It has been said that medieval thinkers philosophized on their knees, but, bolstered by the new studies, they dared to stand up and to rise to full stature."[28] Humanism gave people the tools to stand with courage and conviction where before they had cowered with uncertainty and fear before a feudal lord or military dictator. This was an important shift, as people were emboldened to read and reason for themselves. The flame of liberty was once again nearing the reach of the common people.

This period was an important predecessor to what came next: the Enlightenment. The Renaissance paved the way for Enlightenment thinkers and philosophers to question the divine right of kings; to insist that humankind was capable of self-government; and to prove that God intended for humans to be free of tyranny and anarchy. Something better was possible.

By the mid-eighteenth century, after the outbreak of a scientific revolution in many parts of Europe, France had become the locus of thought and discussion, and thus the birthplace of the Enlightenment. Whereas reason and religion had been two foci of the Renaissance, during the Enlightenment the focus spread to include science and government. America's Founders were full fruits of the Enlightenment, and it is no coincidence that many of them were also, in their own right, as much scientists as philosophers and statesmen.

In America at the peak of the Enlightenment, at last the key ingredients of liberty were found all existing at the same place and time and in a way such as had never before existed. It was almost too good to be true: a virtuous and moral people; widespread education, rooted in the classics; a shared vision of the future; a common language; a geography that lent itself to liberty; and leaders with public virtue, ready to carry the torch of freedom.

But that was not all. Perhaps most importantly, she also had adversity, what author Oliver DeMille calls the "one thing all great civilizations in history have in common."[29] That adversity would come in abundance, and in its wake would arise some of the best and bravest bearers of the torch of liberty the world has ever known.

It is essential that those of us today who seek to carry on the torch understand and appreciate this critical period. In many ways, it mirrors the opportunities and challenges of our time. In bears many lessons that we must study and understand in order to step forward and qualify ourselves to be among those who pass on the torch of liberty.

CHAPTER 21

THE MAN WHO KEPT MOVING FORWARD

It had been a good day—in fact, one of the happiest he had known. He sat, surrounded by friends young and old. The Wampanoag were there as well to join in the festivities. They had brought deer and turkey, and the celebration and feast had been truly magnificent. It felt good to be full, physically and emotionally.

He had been so empty of late. He wasn't prone to dwell on the past; he had learned early in life that the past could neither be changed nor altered, and it was better to move forward. And that's what he had always done.

His father, his mother, and his grandfather had all died before he reached the age of eight, leaving him an orphan in his uncle's care. And what had he done then? Moved forward. He'd been plagued by illness in his youth, prohibiting him from regular school attendance and enjoyment of the things his friends enjoyed. What had he done then? Moved forward. His early interest in the Bible had led to his association with the Separatist movement. His only surviving relatives, an uncle and a sister, were greatly displeased with this. But what had he done? Moved forward. That was his way. When the Separatists went to Amsterdam and then a year later to Leiden in South Holland, he had gone with them, never looking back.

Well, that's wasn't quite right. He *had* looked back. There was a young woman he'd left in Amsterdam, very young, and he'd never forgotten her. As soon as she turned sixteen, he returned to Amsterdam, and he married that girl. She'd brought light and joy to his life, and together they created the first real family he'd known.

Within two years they had a son, John. Leaving him had been one of the hardest things he'd ever done, but he didn't regret leaving him in the safety of an established country in the arms of trusted friends. Not with what had happened after that. By 1620 the group of Separatists were ready to travel to the new land, a place where they could worship as they wished, freely, without interference. He and his wife had longed for that, and so with sorrowful good-byes and the promise to send for John later, they boarded ship on the *Mayflower*.

They faced a month of delays on land and two months at sea, but finally their new home was within sight. Plagued by approaching winter storms, their original plans foiled, he and other members of that first exploration party took a small boat inland, and after three trips ashore, they finally found a fit site for their new colony.

The crew returned with excitement, anxious to tell their families they could begin to settle the new land, but that dark angel of death that had plagued his childhood had followed him across the ocean. While he was away, his wife had slipped and fallen into the sea's dark depths, never to be recovered. She was gone. He mourned;

he questioned; he knew he would never forget. And then as he had always done, he moved forward.

And that is what I shall continue to do, he told himself. That had been years ago, and today was a new day. He smiled at his new bride, the widow Alice Southworth, and those who had come to celebrate with them. Though life was far from what he might have hoped, still it had been full of good things. There was giving, and there was taking. There was life, and there was death. And he was content in knowing that whatever might come, he could face it, God at his side and hope in his heart, and he would keep moving forward.

William Bradford, that widower-groom, became the second governor of Plymouth Plantation when the first governor, John Carver, died of a sudden illness. Carver had been among the nearly 50 percent of the colony who did not survive the first winter. Disease, encounters with hostile Indians, the harshness of winter, and the short supply of food and other necessary supplies cost many their lives. Shortly after Carver's death Bradford was appointed second governor of the infant colony, and he was reelected every year thereafter until his death, serving as governor every year except the few years when he declined to do so.

Even before they landed in Plymouth, they had agreed to be ruled by a written document, the Mayflower Compact, which became America's first constitutional document. That document served as a foundation for their society, and upon its principles Bradford built the pilgrim society. Once the initial years of hardship were over, Bradford created a system of working fields and sharing produce and developed a charter allowing for ownership of land after seven years of service.

Bradford developed a friendship with an Indian, Squanto, who is himself worthy of study. Squanto taught the pilgrims how to plant and prepare their fields and how to fish. He also served as their guide and interpreter to the Indian neighbors. Squanto's invaluable assistance helped move the pilgrims from bare survival to more prosperous conditions, and the first Thanksgiving recorded was likely due in great part to the pilgrims following the planting and harvesting methods Squanto shared with them.

Long had the pilgrims faced religious persecution, and those early men and women made great sacrifices to ensure their posterity enjoyed a right to worship as they wished. Bradford's gravestone reads, "Qua patres difficillime adepti sunt nolite turpiter relinquere," or "What our forefathers with so much difficulty secured, do not basely relinquish."

Bradford left the comforts of a well-established society and risked everything he had to help establish a colony where religious truth and social liberty were valued and protected. He serves as an example of a great leader who courageously overcame adversity and passed the torch of freedom forward in time.

LESSONS FROM WILLIAM BRADFORD ON HOW TO PASS THE TORCH

1. The word *pilgrim* means "sojourner," "stranger," or "exile." Bradford's life serves to remind us that passing the torch of freedom isn't an easy act, nor can it be done alone. The pilgrims succeeded in establishing a new land of liberty because they fought, lived, dreamt, and died together. They were united by a common constitution and vision. Their unity and family-based society allowed them to succeed where other attempted colonies had failed.

2. Another reason the Plymouth Colony succeeded is because the people recognized they would not survive without God as necessary part of their society. The simple Mayflower Compact reminds us of this: "mutually in the Presence of God and one of another, [we] covenant and combine ourselves together into a civil Body Politick, for our better Ordering and Preservation, and Furtherance of the Ends aforesaid; And by Virtue hereof to enact, constitute, and frame, such just and equal Laws, Ordinances, Acts, Constitutions and Offices, from time to time, as shall be thought most meet and convenient for the General good of the Colony; unto which we promise all due submission and obedience."

CHAPTER 22

THE PURITAN MOSES

"A letter for you, Commander; just arrived by post." The young soldier placed the epistle on the commander's desk and turned to leave.

"Thank you," the commander replied. "Please return in ten minutes, and I shall have a response. I wish it to be sent right away."

"We'll hold the post then, sir," the young man replied.

With anxious hands the commander grasped the letter. *Good news or ill?* he wondered to himself. Only months before his pen had been among those who signed the death warrant for the king. As a result King Charles had been executed, and since then his life had been a whirlwind of military and political upheaval. He had hoped to be home by Christmas, but today was Christmas Eve, and he was still miles from home. He had been sent to Ireland to quell the royalist uprising there. So far he had been favored with victory, and soon, he felt, his tasks here would be over.

He smiled when he saw the small, simple handwriting. The letter was from his wife! Together they had had nine children, six sons and three daughters. One had died in infancy, and two others of illness. He paused to offer a prayer for his family before reading the brief letter she had posted. His eyes shut tight, and his lips moved soundlessly. "Please Lord, keep them safe and in thy watchful care; prosper and defend them!"

Then with rapidly beating heart he opened her letter. He couldn't help but worry about them while he was away. With a prayer of gratitude he reread her last lines: "Truly my life is but half a life in your absence. Did not the Lord make it up himself, which I must acknowledge to the praise of his grace. God speed on your journey home."

Quickly he scrawled a response: "Dearest, I could not satisfy myself to omit this post, although I have not much to write…. The Lord bless all thy good counsel and example to all those about thee, and hear all thy prayers and accept thee always. Yours—Oliver." Surely he had been blessed in his choice of wife. She was a constant friend and support to him, and how he had needed it throughout the past few years!

It had been less than a decade since he, Oliver Cromwell, had aligned himself with the parliamentarians. Religious persecution at the time had grown intense, and political corruption was at a peak. Every day one person or another was found guilty of some religious or political crime for which he could see no real grounds. As a landowner, he had personally experienced the oppressive taxes imposed by King Charles and was subject to heavy fines levied by those seeking power. Supporting his widowed mother, his wife, and his children had been nearly impossible at times, even though he, unlike many around him, owned land and collected rent.

Those in Parliament were all landowners. He was among them, and he saw in their midst much corruption. The poorer subjects of the land had no representation and virtually no real legal protection; the kingdom was disintegrating, and revolt was imminent. The king's men were in favor of one common church, but Cromwell opposed that policy, seeing no reason why everyone should be forced to believe the same thing.

Religious persecution and unrest grew, and so early in 1642 when civil war ensued and Parliament began to raise troops against the king, he was quick to join the side of Parliament. He had no military experience and was first placed as a captain over a small body of mounted troops.

Despite his inexperience he found early success, and within a year was promoted to colonel. Less than three years later he was second in command of the Parliament's most effective and largest army. From there, successes in Ireland and beyond led to his appointment as Lord-General over the entire parliamentary forces. Some wondered at his quick rise to eminence, but Cromwell was not surprised. A religious experience early on in his military career had won his soul to Christianity, and ever after he felt his military and political victories were a direct result of God's favor and will.

Not long after that Christmastime letter to his wife, Cromwell quelled the royalist rebellions in Scotland. He returned home and helped set up a commonwealth, eventually becoming head of the commonwealth and Lord Protector in 1653. He was offered the role of monarch but refused, stating, "I would not seek to set up that which Providence hath destroyed and laid in the dust, and I would not build Jericho again."[30] He felt God preferred he be bound by a written constitution and that he rule hand in hand with Parliament.

Through these methods he gradually eliminated the unrest and turmoil that had before been the order of the day. Religious persecution was greatly curtailed, and for the first time in four hundred years the Jews were allowed to reenter England and worship at the synagogues there. At the same time Cromwell established England as a dominant sea power and in less than five years created a naval strategy that prepared England's economy to flourish in ensuing years.

This period of reformation was short-lived, however. Cromwell died of an illness within five years, and within three years after his death the monarchy was restored. Charles II assumed the throne, and religious persecution began to again increase. During the reigns of King Charles II and James II, Presbyterianism was not tolerated. The freedom of religion the Presbyterians had known under Cromwell was obliterated, so many of them sought for a new peace by fleeing to America.

Oliver Cromwell's achievements are not without controversy. While his accomplishments and rise to power are extraordinary, he has also been the subject of criticism for his treatment of Catholics and certain other measures. In considering his life and motivations, it's helpful to also consider the times in which he lived and the circumstances that shaped the world he grew up in.

From this perspective, in many ways Cromwell headed a tolerant, inclusive, and largely civilian regime and sought to restore order and stability at home. While he was not perfect, his contributions established a precedent for parliamentary, constitutional rule, and it can justly be said he was a soldier-statesman who put an end to civil war and restored peace at home and respect abroad.

LESSONS FROM OLIVER CROMWELL ON HOW TO PASS THE TORCH

1. Cromwell lived during a period of many other influential writers and thinkers, among them John Locke, John Milton (who served as Cromwell's secretary), and John Owen, known as the greatest Puritan theologian, who served as Cromwell's army chaplain. These great thinkers likely influenced each other, and studying their ideas together lends insight into this important period and the events that occurred incident to their leadership.

2. The life and times of Cromwell illustrate that the cycle of decline quickly bleeds into the cycle of growth and then back into the cycle of decline. Without a foundation of morality and education, along with necessary governmental forms, checks and balances, long-term political stability cannot be achieved. When freedom is attacked, pay attention to the state of those same factors.

CHAPTER 23

THE PRINCE OF LETTERS

66 **I**t is good to see you, Samuel!" The frail woman's admiration was plainly evident, and as she stretched out her hands to greet her friend, the elderly man's smile matched her own.

"Lady Kenmure, it is always a pleasure." He grasped her hands tightly and sat in a nearby chair.

"The tide has turned, it seems," the woman said. "For so long have your priestly letters been a comfort and aid to me in my darkest hours; your shepherding and words of Christ have been my greatest solace. Now you come seeking help from me. I can hardly comprehend it, Samuel."

Her friend's eyes were drawn to the ground momentarily, and then he met her gaze. "It will be a privilege, should they take me, Lady Kenmure, a privilege to give my life for Christ. What greater gift could I give to One who has given so much for me?"

The woman's eyes suddenly filled with tears. "Samuel, is it really that bad? Is what they say true?"

He laughed. "What 'they' say is never true, and no, it isn't that bad, though it saddens me deeply." He looked out toward an open window and then continued, "With the monarchy restored, I haven't much hope, have I? Not after *Lex, Rex*."

The woman smiled. "You were never one to hold your tongue when you felt strongly about something, that is true. And the king isn't likely to forget that your writings disinherit him of his power."

"And I am proud of it," came his quick response. "Though I am imperfect, I have always tried to defend the truth. And my reward? King Charles has generously charged me with treason." His voice began to break, but he went on. "I have been deprived of my church, my university chair, and my stipend."

"No, Samuel!" The woman cried out.

"*Lex, Rex*," Samuel informed her, "by decree of the king, shall be burned, my presbytery overthrown—I am under house arrest! But I had to visit my flock once more before they arrived to enforce my punishment." The woman's face was covered in tears. "I'll likely be hanged," he finished.

Lady Kenmure marveled at the total lack of fear or worry on Samuel's part.

"That has been the fate of the most prominent covenant leaders here, and for better or worse I am counted among those. It is only a matter of time," he mused. "But truly, it will be a privilege to die for Christ. I could ask for no worthier gift for Him than my life, after all."

The woman shook her head, and he stood to go. "I must be on my way. I have many more I wish to visit!"

She asked, "How has Jean taken it? And your daughter?"

"Ah, my wife…she will endure. She is a strong one. And Agnes—she takes after her mother. She will be fine. But that is why I have come, Lady Kenmure. Should I be taken, would you look after them?" At these words Samuel's own eyes filled with tears. "I would thank you most kindly for it! That would be my only regret, to leave them alone. It would be a great comfort to me to know they are in your care!"

"Of course, Samuel!" she replied. "Of course! It's the least I can do!"

"Thank you, friend. You are in my prayers; God watches over His sheep and will not leave us comfortless. God be with you!" And with that, the elderly preacher turned and disappeared into the night.

Samuel Rutherford, the friend and confidant of many Scottish and international intellectual and Christian elite, as well as the peasants and farmers whose lives he touched, was the foe of the monarchy, the "Resolutioners" who supported the return to power of Charles II in 1660. Rutherford's name was known near and far and was almost synonymous with piety and with something less innocuous, a dangerous idea that "all men are created equal."

Rutherford was the first to connect the idea of natural law, or self-evident laws by which nature and people are governed, with scriptural revelation. As a result of this connection, he wrote, government should be limited. The scriptures were clear. God gave power to humanity, and humans then appointed rulers. This was a far cry from the belief of monarchists in that day, who believed God gave power to kings to use as they would upon their lesser subjects who were *not* ordained kings.

"Every man," he wrote, "by nature is a freeman born; by nature, no man cometh out of the womb under any civil subjection to king, prince, or judge." That was the main subject of one of his most prominent works, *Lex, Rex*, subtitled *The Law and the Prince*, advocating limited government and constitutionalism—the work for which he would be convicted of treason and condemned to death.

This unique perspective of the equality of men was in many ways groundbreaking, and his writings on government had a great impact on the American Founders' ideas on civil and religious liberty. The ideas of rule of law and nature's law can be directly traced to his writings.

Rutherford's perspectives and piety were the fruit of great opposition and sorrow. He was preceded in death by his first wife, his parents, and eight of his own children, with only one child surviving him. He also lived as an exile earlier in his life for his "heretical" teachings. His first pastorate was over a rural Scottish flock which he grew to love dearly. Farmers and peasants packed the seats of his church when he was at the pulpit, and word of his beautiful sermons spread far as he became a pastor-celebrity.

Being exiled from his flock and forbidden to preach for a time was a source of immense sorrow for him, one that, he wrote, almost "broke my faith in two halves." Yet, in retrospect he wrote that even that experience had brought him to know Christ and be comforted of Him in a greater way than he had ever before known, and that there were no words to express the kindness Christ had given him in the midst of his deepest trials. His own trials allowed him to strengthen those around him in powerful ways, which he frequently did through writing encouraging letters to family, friends, and associates. As a result of his voluminous, encouraging, Christ-centered works, he has been called "the prince of letter writers."

Samuel Rutherford's name has been forgotten by history, but his influence has spanned the ages down to our present day. The equality of humankind and the concept of natural law are ideas found in the both the Declaration of Independence and the US Constitution, and they are ideas for which we should always remember his name. Perhaps just as important are his ecclesiastical writings, which remind us that liberty has its roots in morality and knowledge and that sound government is based on a deep understanding of the word of God.

LESSONS FROM SAMUEL RUTHERFORD ON HOW TO PASS THE TORCH

1. If we don't understand the *roots* of freedom, we will lose the *fruits* of those ideas as well. Who today can name the originator of the phrase, "all men are created equal"? If we cannot name Samuel Rutherford as the early author of that phrase, then how well do we understand the idea itself, and how capable are we of defending and passing on that idea? Those who would pass the torch of liberty must resist the forces of today that would cause us to forget the past, carrying us away in a river of entertainment and revisionist history that adds little to our souls and nothing to our liberty.

2. Both John Locke and Algernon Sydney were born during Rutherford's time and were surely influenced by his writings and teachings. Those who pass the torch often do so both through influencing peers and through contributing to words and works that stand the test of time.

CHAPTER 24

THE TYRANT'S ENEMY

This is the book, the young man said to himself. He reverently fingered the corners of the volume. He had promised himself he would wait for this day, the day he turned fifteen, to read it.

As he looked at the work, he thought back on the past few years. He couldn't remember the knock on the door, or the news brought by messenger of his father's death—after all, he'd been only three when it happened. He did faintly remember standing at the harbor with his mother, the cold spring wind tossing waves high, watching the ship inch its way forward. He remembered seeing the body, wrapped in a sheet, carried respectfully ashore.

The ship was in sight of the harbor when it had happened, they'd been told. His father, sick with tuberculosis, had grown worse and worse on the trip back from England. When he did not improve and he suspected the worst, his father had carefully prepared his own will. There, not far from the harbor, he had passed away, leaving Josiah fatherless, and his mother a widow.

"I give to my son, Josiah Quincy, when he shall have arrived at the age of fifteen years, Algernon Sydney's works." That is what his father's will had read. He'd also bequeathed him John Locke's writings, Lord Bacon's, and a handful of others. "May the spirit of liberty rest upon him!" were his father's final written words to him.

He remembered how they had placed his father's library of books in a warehouse for safekeeping until he was old enough to read them. Sadly, however, the warehouse had caught fire; everything had been burnt. That had only deepened Josiah's resolve to read the books valued so highly by his father, and in expectation of his fifteenth birthday he had carefully procured each work he would have received on that day.

Josiah had heard John Adams say that the principles of America's founding rested in large part on Sidney's works. Jefferson had conceded that in Locke's and Sidney's writings were found the roots of the Founders' view of liberty. This was the author they spoke of! Josiah's pulse raced as he anxiously opened the text and began to read. Late into the night he read; then early the next morning he awoke and resumed his studies. Gradually in his mind's eye the life of the English politician began to take shape.

Born in England in Baynard's Castle in 1623, Sidney Algernon belonged to a wealthy family. He was well educated and well spoken and was known in his youth for his quick wit and sweet nature. He showed great courage as a combatant in the battle of Marston Moor and then later in speaking out against King Charles II, who ascended the throne following the death of Oliver Cromwell.

Sidney believed strongly in ideas that went against a traditional monarchical view of government. "Monarchy," he once wrote, "is the worst evil that can befall a nation." His views were informed by the tumultuous times in which he lived, as he had witnessed firsthand the evils of monarchy and the civil wars and corruption that resulted from the battle for the throne. In his most famous work,

Discourses Concerning Government, Sidney detailed the importance of a limited-mixed government, the necessity of the consent of the people for any leader to assume power, and the right of people to alter or abolish a government that has become tyrannical.

Shortly after King Charles II's rise to power, Sidney was implicated in a plot to kill the king. Only one witness could be found, but two witnesses were necessary to try him. The controversial trial that followed, led by Lord Chief Justice Jeffreys, included his ruling that "to write is to act."

Because Sidney had written about revolution, Jeffreys argued, he had in effect acted in rebellion against the king. Therefore Sidney's own *Discourses Concerning Government* was used as the second witness required to try him. Though his *Discourses* spoke about government and rebellion in general terms, Sidney's words were twisted to be a direct attack on Charles II's throne. Sidney responded, "If you take the scripture to pieces…you may accuse David of saying there is no God and of the Apostles that they were drunk." Nevertheless, Sidney's twisted words were used against him, and he was found guilty of treason.

Sidney, familiar with legal methods of the day, attempted to defend himself by demonstrating the many points whereon his trial had been biased and illegally performed, but all to no avail. After five months of imprisonment, Sidney was brought to the scaffold. "We live in an age that makes truth pass for treason," he said to the sheriff and those present before his hanging. "I am persuaded… God had left nations to the liberty of setting up such governments as best pleased themselves, and that magistrates were set up for the good of nations, not nations for the glory of magistrates…. Grant that I may die glorifying…that Old Cause in which I was from my youth engaged." With those words the great politician surrendered his life.

Though he died in infamy, the power of his words lived on and later bore fruit in both the Declaration of Independence and the US Constitution. Josiah Quincy, after decades of studying those works recommended to him by his father, wrote, "The principles those writings inculcate have been during my whole life among my chiefest studies, not more out of respect of the recommendation of my father, than from my perception of their truth and intrinsic excellence, and my conviction that on their prevalence the happiness and prosperity of every society depend."[31]

Truly freedom, happiness, and prosperity rest on knowing and understanding the words and works of Algernon Sidney and those like him. They sacrificed their very lives that the torch of liberty might burn brightly down through the generations and inspire those who follow to remember their sacrifices and follow in their steps.

LESSONS FROM ALGERNON SIDNEY ON HOW TO PASS THE TORCH

1. The time in which Sidney lived was one of immense oppression of liberties after the English civil wars. This period caused a great number of men to rise up who stood for principles of natural liberty. Like Sidney, each of them risked everything in defense of these sacred truths. Those who passed the torch of freedom have been largely forgotten today; their names, as well as their ideas, are no longer discussed or studied. As we see the number of attacks on our freedom increase daily, our response, like those of old, should be to renew our study of previous torchbearers and expand our understanding of liberty. Though liberty is momentarily silenced, as long as torchbearers continue to arise, there is hope of future freedom.

2. In setting up the US Constitution, the American revolutionaries were not tinkering with governmental theory. Rather, they were preserving past liberties gained by those who had previously carried the torch of freedom forward. Studying the classics gave the Founders great courage to face the challenges of their time and tools for successfully defending liberty. We must understand the ideas and ideals of the torch of freedom if it is to be preserved and its truths are to remain fresh in our day.

CHAPTER 25

FRIEND OF SLAVE AND FOE OF KING

A warm July breeze wafted through the open window, providing little relief from the oppressive summer heat. The man at the desk tugged at his collar uncomfortably and wiped his brow with a wilted handkerchief. His tall, thin figure bent over a book. "I know not which is worst," he read quietly to himself, "to be gnawed to death by Rats, or devoured by a Lion."

"Humph," he sighed aloud. Which was worse? Tyranny, or anarchy? The lion of monarchy, or the "rats" of pure democracy? He'd been studying Tyrrell's *Patriarcha non monarcha* for months and found in this man's words a source of inspiration. A costly inspiration.

A clamor began to rise in the courtyard below, growing increasingly disruptive. "These God-forsaken doctrines *will* be burned! And unless you would join them, Thomas, it's best you leave us be! By order of the university!"

The man at the desk turned pale. Quickly he moved to the window's edge, being careful to remain unseen. Cautiously he peered through the window. He could see a group passing below.

There was Thomas James, the astute librarian. He took his job as chief librarian quite seriously and was obviously upset. Ahead of him was a short line of men, arms full of books, walking toward the Bodleian Quadrangle. *So it is happening after all!* The man had read Oxford University's decree earlier that month "against certain pernicious books and damnable doctrines" and the ensuing order to publicly burn the works of Hobbes, Milton, Tyrrell, and others. But he'd hoped it would all pass over, that somehow the decree would be forgotten. Of course it had only been a hope.

He glanced across the room at the bookshelves lining his wall, a wild fear rising inside him. Since Oliver Cromwell's rule forty years before, book burnings were a real threat to those who spoke out against anyone who was in power. He'd heard of it happening before, but this time was different. This time he owned the very works he saw them carrying away; this time his own manuscripts could well be fit for inclusion in the bonfire.

Quickly he crossed the room and checked the lock of his door; it was secure. Then he crossed back to the window and drew the curtains. From a dresser drawer he pulled out a heavy canvas bag and carefully placed in it the sheaf of handwritten notes which comprised his manuscripts, along with two volumes of Tyrrell's *Patriarcha*. Where would they be safe? Where would he be safe?

Anxiously he waited for nightfall, too fearful to eat, too nervous to read or write, and too distraught to do anything but worry about the future. *Where would he go? Who would care where he went?* His dear friend, the Earl of Shaftesbury, had died in refuge in Holland only a year before. He himself now lived in the earl's Exeter House at Oxford. Would he, too, be forced abroad? One thing was clear, he was no longer safe in England.

Bang, bang, bang! The stillness of the night was broken by a thunderous pounding. "Let us in, you fool!" There was no response. The voice rang out again: "Locke! John Locke! Open the door! You're wanted for high treason!"

Within moments the door was battered down. Inside, in perfect order, were Locke's belongings, minus Locke, his manuscripts, and his copies of Tyrrell. Miles away, he was well on his journey to Rotterdam, where he would continue to write against tyranny in all its forms as long as he had breath.

John Locke was born during a tumultuous period when representative government was hotly contested and the traditional systems that supported feudalism and monarchy were under attack. He was seventeen when Charles I was executed, and he witnessed Oliver Cromwell's subsequent rise to power. Upon Cromwell's death, power was wrested from the people back into the grasp of a king.

Locke watched these events closely, and his writings were shaped by the patterns of history he saw unfolding in England. After graduating from Oxford, he began studying medicine, and during that time he met the Earl of Shaftesbury, who would have a great influence on his life's direction. He became the earl's personal physician and personally oversaw his medical needs and procedures.

By 1681 Charles II had dissolved Parliament altogether, intending, it seemed, never to summon them back. Shaftesbury, with Locke at his side, stood in the crossfire as Charles's most dangerous opponent, and when the king's attacks on his opponents intensified, Shaftesbury sought refuge in Holland, only to die there two months after arriving.

It was then that Locke, who had been staying in England, realized his own life was at risk. He too fled to Holland, with an extradition for trial and hanging issued on his heels. A tumultuous decade followed, and at its close Prince William of Orange assumed the English throne. With his ascension, parliamentary rule and Protestant succession were secured. Locke returned to England at last, safe to write and move about the country. Still fearful of repercussions, he published his two treatises on government anonymously.

John Locke's ideas were clear and, he believed, nonnegotiable. People, not rulers, are sovereign; government cannot take the property of people without their consent, and therefore taxes must not be raised on a people without their consent. Slavery puts people into a state of war, and people tyrannized by their government have a right to "resume their original liberty" and throw off such a government. These and other ideas fueled the flame of liberty, and his *Essay Concerning Human Understanding* placed him among England's philosophical elite. He died a bachelor, in relative ease and renown, at age seventy-two.

Locke's name has become synonymous with concepts of natural law, liberty, and private property, ideas upon which American's founding heavily rested. His influence is prominent in both the Declaration of Independence and the US Constitution.

Underlying all his writings is the idea of a fundamental moral order guaranteeing each person rights to life, liberty, and private property. Because of that order, according to Locke, governments that abuse those rights are tyrannical and have no legitimate authority, be they monarchy, democracy, or any government in between. He firmly believed that the political and social worlds are governed by natural laws as certain and universal as those which govern the physical world.

After Locke's death his influence was spread far and wide, first by two English radicals, John Trenchard and Thomas Gordon, and then by Voltaire and later Montesquieu. In the Western world Locke seemed everywhere spoken of, debated, and considered. However, Locke's ideas vanished over time, replaced by a conservative reaction in Europe in response to the Napoleonic Wars and forgotten through the passage of time in America.

Despite the years that have passed and his near-erasure from commonly studied history, Locke's influence on those who formed our country is uncontestable. The Founders' writings and ideas clearly demonstrate Locke's heavy influence. All humans are born with equal rights to life, liberty, and property; government's role is to protect those rights, and when it fails to do so and instead attacks them, it must be abolished. Natural law declares freedom to be people's right and their heritage.

Locke's legacy is great, and his call is clear: those who value liberty must study her roots and defend her principles, or tyranny is the only result.

LESSONS FROM JOHN LOCKE ON HOW TO PASS THE TORCH

1. When rights to life, liberty, and property are under attack, tyranny and bondage are not far away. Locke understood that the roots of liberty extend from recognizing basic essential rights. Today's world obscures the recognition of those rights and makes their source even more obscure. To pass on the torch of freedom, we must recognize everyone's inalienable rights and also agree on their source. That is where liberty begins and ends.

2. To some extent, every society in each generation is required to apply the principles of freedom afresh to their own circumstances and unique challenges. This is impossible to do without understanding the thinkers on liberty—prominent among them John Locke and Algernon Sidney. It's not enough to know their names and when they lived. A revival of fluency in understanding their works, coupled with the ability to apply the principles they spoke of, is needed to ensure our freedoms are not lost.

CHAPTER 26

AMERICA'S GREATEST THINKER

"**J**onathan!" A girl of fourteen years stood in knee-high grass, looking out over the fields. Hearing no response, she let out an exasperated sigh. "Jonathan!" she called again. Still there was nothing.

She spoke to her younger companion, Mary. "We should never have taught him how to read!"

Mary laughed. "That's only half the problem. This is the other half." She spread her arms wide, indicating the view around them, then she let out a small squeal. "Agh! Aggggh!" She wildly brushed off the body of a large spider that was dangling from her hair. "And *this* most particularly is the problem! *I hate spiders!*" Her whole body shook in fear.

Her elder sister, Ann, quickly brushed the spider from its roost, and it flew away in the wind. "Why on earth does he love spiders so much? It's disgusting!"

Suddenly the young man burst through the grass behind them. "There you are!" Ann's voice had an edge to it that made him instantly wish he was anywhere but there. "The cow needs to be milked, and you promised Mother you'd be home hours ago!"

Suddenly Mary noticed what was in his hands: a long stick. That could only mean one thing. "You put that down right now, Jonathan!" She cast a fearful glance toward the end of the stick, and sure enough, a large spider dangled from a silky thread.

The boy's eyes were suddenly lit with mischief. "I shall not put it down! This spider is part of my scientific study and is a valuable specimen!"

Ann shook a finger at her younger brother. "You and your specimens! You're always bringing them home, and you know Mother said to leave them in their natural habitat!"

She was right. Mother *had* insisted he not bring any more spiders home.

"But I know what makes a spider fly!" Ann and Mary eyed him cautiously, but he could tell he had their interest, so he rushed on. "I know you don't like spiders, but truly nothing is more wonderful than the spider! Look." He gently let the spider down upon a long stalk of grass. "Watch closely!"

He began tapping the stalk, and with each jolt the spider's body shook. Suddenly the spider launched into the wind. "Look! Look! Look at its tail—the web comes from its tail, and because it's lighter than the wind, it flies upward, drawing the spider after it!" The girls, slightly appalled, were also fascinated.

"Do you see those trees?" He pointed to a grove not far from where they stood. "When the web catches on them, or on anything really, the spider will have a new home. Or perhaps it will move on from those trees to the next grove. It can go wherever it wants, really, flying on the wind. Wouldn't you like to be a spider?"

Mary remembered it was spiders they were talking about. "No, I would not! I hate spiders!"

Ann laughed and then tugged on Jonathan's sleeve. "That's enough spiders for one day, Jonathan Edwards. The cow doesn't care what your excuse is, you've made her wait long enough."

"Aw, all right," he conceded, and the young arachnologist headed home.

That boy-naturalist, though his name has been forgotten by most of us today, would grow to great influence, playing a key role in launching America's first Great Awakening and becoming one of the most brilliant American intellects who ever lived.

Born in 1703, he was the only son of the ten children his mother bore. His four older sisters doted on him, and—following after their mother—each developed a keen intellect. Under his father's and sisters' tutelage the precocious boy began studying Latin at age six. Before he entered Yale just after his thirteenth birthday, he had a solid grasp of Latin, Greek, and Hebrew. At age eleven he composed a scientific essay, "The Flying Spider," detailing his observations on the ballooning behavior of spiders.

Throughout his life his scientific bent was matched only by his religious convictions. His "Flying Spider" work ends with a "Corollary" section which details the goodness of the Creator as demonstrated through the habits of flying spiders and through all of nature. For Edwards, science always bolstered his conviction of God's existence and influence, and throughout his life, Edwards turned to nature to pray, find solace, and spend time with the Creator.

His early academic success continued, and by the age of four-teen he found one of the greatest influences of his personal and academic career: John Locke. Before his death he confessed of Locke's *Essay Concerning Human Understanding*, "I was as much engaged, and had more satisfaction and pleasure in studying it, than the most greedy miser in gathering up handfuls of silver and gold from some new-discovered treasure."

Before the age of twenty he had graduated and assumed a pastorate, and it was during his time as a pastor that the bulk of his writing took place. He wrote over seventy-one resolutions, and his influence in speaking and writing resulted in thousands of conversions.

His words and works laid the foundation for those who followed and prepared people's mind to recognize the unfair taxation and representation that England had imposed. Without Edwards' influence, and other proponents of the Great Awakening, the American Revolution would never have come to fruition, and the resulting Declaration of Independence and Constitution would never have materialized. His final years were spent as a missionary with the Mohawks and Mohicans.

Among Edwards' descendants are more than three hundred clergymen, missionaries, and theological professors; 120 college professors; 110 lawyers, sixty physicians, thirty judges, fourteen university presidents, three US senators, and one US vice president. His writings and sermons had great influence in his day and beyond, which in turn shaped the thinking of the American Founders. Jonathan Edwards' name is virtually unknown today, but his influence is still felt.

As with many of those who passed the torch of liberty forward, his actions live on and compel us to reexamine the forgotten past and learn the truths he dedicated his life to sharing.

LESSONS FROM JONATHAN EDWARDS ON HOW TO PASS THE TORCH

1. Jonathan Edwards' life demonstrates both the impact of an excellent education and the weakness of our own educational system today in preparing thinking men and women. His fluency in languages and classics and his deep biblical understanding bore lasting fruit that prepared future generations for impact. To have the same impact and carry on the torch, we must similarly pay the price for an excellent education.

2. The first Great Awakening was a period of intense religious revival which opened people's minds to new ways of thinking. Without Edwards' influence the impact of first Great Awakening would have been much more limited. We need a similar revival of recognition of God and His hand in our past and present, and we need men and women of Jonathan Edwards' caliber to stand up and lead the next awakening.

THE GREAT ITINERANT

66 "**T**his is incredible!" Benjamin Franklin had never before seen the city of Philadelphia ablaze with so much activity and excitement. He watched the crowds pass from the top floor of his two-story home. It was not yet seven in the morning, but the steady stream of people had commenced an hour or two earlier.

"They say he has preached to crowds of tens of thousands in England, and was heard clearly by all! Can you believe it, Father?"

Franklin shook his head. "'They' say a thousand things that have no basis in truth. I have no doubt that half the things we have heard about him are complete fabrication, William." He shook his head adamantly. "No, I don't believe it."

"Please, Father, let us go! Everyone else is there or has heard him before."

Though the crowds looked oppressive, the thought of seeing the preacher firsthand was hard to resist. Franklin sighed. "All right, all right. Let us go and view the spectacle."

"Hooray!" William let out a shout of glee.

They slowly made their way to the square. The event was to take place at the courthouse, and Benjamin and his son inched along the edges of the crowd toward the preacher.

"We'll never hear from this far back," Benjamin muttered, "Follow me!" he grasped his son's hand tightly. The crowd was pressed tight, but by the time the preacher assumed his post at the top of the stairs, the Franklins had found a spot not far from them.

"Is that him, Father?"

"Yes, I believe it is." The young man they spoke of was not much to look at. Only twenty-five years old, he was pale and appeared weak and sickly. His hair flew wildly about in every direction; he was cross-eyed and disappointingly small.

The man began to speak, and as if by a magic spell, the roar of the crowd fell to a hush. To Franklin's astonishment, the man's voice seemed to fill the entire square. On a whim he turned to his son. "Stay right here, William. I'll be back."

His son didn't blink, entranced at the preacher's theatrics. "Yes, Father," he mumbled in reply.

Franklin smiled and picked his way back out of the crowd. It was easier to move between the press of bodies now that they were listening intently to the preacher. He headed toward his shop on Market Street, counting each block, his astonishment increasing with each step. The preacher's voice rang distinctly far beyond the edges of the crowd, and Franklin walked until he could no longer hear the voice.

He stopped and calculated. "Thirty thousand people!" Franklin's amazement continued the next day as he observed a "wonderful…change soon made in the manners of the inhabitants [of Philadelphia]. From being thoughtless or indifferent about religion, it seemed as if all the world were growing religious, so that one could not walk thro' the town in an evening without hearing psalms sung in different families of every street."[32]

George Whitefield always knew that he loved life in the limelight. A voracious reader of plays from his youth, he was guilty of skipping primary school to participate in theatrical performances. After a conversion experience at college, he translated his love of theater into sermons that included crying, singing, and acting out biblical scenes.

Because his preaching style was so unusual and drew such large crowds, Whitefield took to preaching out of doors, without script or podium, something unusual and unprecedented. His unusual ways and incredible gifts did not go unnoticed. After hearing Whitefield preach, one of England's most famous actors remarked, "I would give a hundred guineas, if I could say 'Oh' like Mr. Whitefield."[33] When he traveled to the American colonies, people flocked to hear what newspapers touted as "the marvel of the age."

Whitefield followed his friends and fellow preachers, the well-known Wesley brothers, to the New World on a missionary trip to Georgia. While there, he founded an orphanage which still exists today as the oldest charity in North America.

Preaching and supporting the orphanage became his two real loves to which he gave his life. Whitefield became the most traveled evangelist of his time. He would arise at 4 a.m. and begin preaching by fix or six in the morning. He would often preach for forty to sixty hours a week and after preaching would experience serious after-effects from having pushed himself so hard.

At a time when international travel was torturous, during his twelve trips to America he traversed more American roads than any other person of his time; he traveled twelve times to Scotland in addition to Ireland, Bermuda, and the Netherlands and is believed to have been heard by more than ten million people. It is also estimated that at least 80 percent of the American colonists heard him preach at one time or another over the course of his travels. His last sermon on his first tour was held at Boston Commons and attracted more than twenty-three thousand, very likely the largest gathering in American history up to that point.

While Whitefield's orations were, by all accounts, mesmerizing, the long-term impact of his influence is just as noteworthy. Whitefield cut across the boundaries of colonies and denominations, creating common ground and preparing the way for religious liberty in the United States.

A secondary result of his preaching was to firmly establish in the minds of colonists the importance of religion and resistance of monarchical and parliamentary influence in local matters. Whitefield almost single-handedly brought about the Great Awakening, a period of religious revival that gave people the courage to resist tyranny and unjust taxation and ultimately prepared the colonies for the founding of a nation.

Whitefield's influence at the time he lived should not be forgotten. The religious revival he initiated and the reformation of thought that resulted were the seedbed that led to the Revolution and the American founding.

LESSONS FROM GEORGE WHITEFIELD ON HOW TO PASS THE TORCH

1. Samuel Adams, influenced by Whitefield, once wrote, "Religion and public liberty are intimately connected and cannot exist separately." The belief that religion and liberty are essential to one another was not an idea held by Adams alone, nor is it one that can long be forgotten without dire implications. A revival in liberty requires a similar revival in religious ideas and principles.

2. George Whitefield was criticized for his showy presentation and what some claimed was nothing more than an effort to get a following. In response to these claims his wife remarked, "A prejudiced person, I know, might say that this is all theatrical artifice and display, but not so will anyone think who has seen and known him."[34] Torchbearers are sometimes the brunt of jokes and unwarranted criticism; some may attack the sincerity of their actions and beliefs, but they are driven by an inner fire that burns despite the winds and waves of resistance.

CHAPTER 28

THE JERSEY FARMER

"Father seems unhappy." The young man spoke to his mother, who was bent over a stove, struggling to light a fire.

The petite woman arose and looked her son in the eyes. "It seems that the college is not quite what he expected," she said.

"Or what he had been promised, you mean!" added a boy of twelve.

"That is true, David," she responded, "but that is none of your affair. Have you finished unpacking the books?"

The boy groaned. "It will take *forever*, Mother! And it's too hot upstairs. I'll die if I have to unpack one more box!"

The woman looked at her son sternly. "You will not die, but consider what your father will say when he comes home if you haven't finished your task. Now go!"

"What will I say?" A booming voice came from the entryway, and the young boy's eyes grew wide. He turned and fled up the stairs. "One small room—can you imagine that, Elizabeth! The entire library of the college fits in one small room!" Her husband's large form filled the kitchen doorway. He was obviously upset.

"But that's the least of my worries," he continued. "Mr. Rush never mentioned the debt; no, he conveniently left that part out. How in the world is such an immense sum to be recovered? And then there are the instructors...why, James here would do a better job than the lot of them!"

The oldest son beamed, but his mother didn't seem quite as pleased. "I don't think that's a good idea, considering he'll be enrolling at the school this fall as a *student*. Moving here wasn't my idea, dear," she responded quietly. "But now that we're here, we must make the best of it, as I know you will."

The newly appointed president of New Jersey College took a deep breath and let it out slowly. "True, true, this wasn't your idea. It was I who dragged you across the ocean, far from family and friends. 'Tis not what we expected, but I think we can turn this school around. In fact, I aim to give Yale and Harvard a fair shake before I'm through."

"Do you?" his wife responded, as she began to knead a loaf of bread.

"The entrance exam is no good. It's got to go. That's the first thing I'll do. Students these days must be able to write Latin prose, and we must see their translations of Virgil and Cicero—and the Greek Gospels of course—before they're admitted. Without a solid foundation in Greek and Latin grammar, they're not ready to learn a thing."

His wife smiled as he continued. He loved preaching, but he loved mentoring as well, and though she hated leaving her loved ones behind in Scotland, she already saw her husband's strengths beginning to shine in this new role. He truly would make an excellent college president.

He continued sharing his plans. "Then there's the fund raising. I've already spoken to Stockton about that. I'm set on raising funds here *and* in Scotland. I believe our friends back home could be persuaded to help out." The man sat on a stool and began peeling an apple while his fuming continued. "A school for training ministers—why, this college isn't good for training mice. But that will change, all right. I aim to mentor the finest leaders this country has seen, in church and beyond!"

"That shouldn't be hard," his wife replied in good humor, "considering there's not much of a country here."

He smiled at her reply. "You'll see," he said. "I expect great things of my school *and* of this country."

John Witherspoon's expectations did not go unmet. Before he retired, he had turned around the College of New Jersey, now known as Princeton University. Within its walls he personally taught or mentored James Madison and Aaron Burr, thirty-seven judges—three of whom became Supreme Court justices—ten Cabinet officers, twelve members of the Continental Congress, twenty-eight US senators, and forty-nine US congressmen.

While Witherspoon's contributions at Princeton are astounding, his impact stretched far beyond the walls of that college. One of his greatest contributions was as a member of the Continental Congress from 1776 to 1782. During that time he staunchly argued for sound economic principles, principles he saw woefully lacking in the early republic. The War of Independence brought with it rapid inflation and price fixing, something he believed would have been avoided had the country adopted a gold standard as he had vehemently advocated. Witherspoon's tremendously sharp mind was matched only by his piety. John Adams said of him, "He was a true son of liberty. So he was. But first, he was a son of the cross."[35]

Witherspoon's dedication to "the cross" shaped his political views as much as his religious ones. He believed strongly that God meant for people to have religious, political, and economic freedom, and he agreed with Locke in proclaiming that the temporal rights to life, liberty, and property were ordained by God. Freedom, he believed, impacted people's souls as well as their pursuit of daily bread.

Many of his views were shaped by a firm conviction that humans have a strong disposition to resist force and escape constraint. Because of this propensity, he felt that enforcing anything, be it good or bad, led to opposition. Therefore, even though he taught that people who did not fear God would do whatever they could get away with until anarchy reigned and fearsome government arose in reaction, he still insisted that people be allowed to believe as they wished without constraint. To Witherspoon, political and spiritual freedom were two sides of the same coin.

Witherspoon's eldest son died in the battle of Germantown in 1777, a casualty of the Revolution. His father and family sacrificed much to the revolutionary cause, from homeland, friends, and family to fortune and a life of ease.

As with each of the Founders, Witherspoon's life reminds us that liberty is a costly endeavor, requiring one's best efforts and most devoted interest.

LESSONS FROM JOHN WITHERSPOON ON HOW TO PASS THE TORCH

1. Witherspoon's life and influence illustrate the impact that biblical principles had on the colonies during the founding era. Witherspoon stated it best: "It is in the man of piety and inward principle that we may expect to find the uncorrupted patriot, the useful citizen, and the invincible soldier. God grant that in America true religion and civil liberty may be inseparable and that the unjust attempts to destroy the one, may in the issue tend to support an establishment of both." As in the founding, so today a return to "piety and principle" is essential in passing the torch of liberty.

2. The impact of Witherspoon's mentorship on the founding generation is hard to accurately estimate. What is clear is that the classics played a huge role in his own education and influence and in the lives of those he mentored. The classics, including the Bible, brought a clarity of principle and conviction that allowed Witherspoon and his students to influence the founding period in many important ways.

PART V

THE AGE OF REVOLUTION

The Renaissance began a chain of events that circled the globe, events that boldly illustrate the cause and effect of various ideas. From politics to music, from art to social norms, no subject and no continent remained unaffected by the influences of liberal ideas and movements. We have seen how the Physical Matrix and Land Matrix are intertwined. Here we begin to witness more clear evidence of the Financial Matrix of control. These three forms of control are in constant opposition to the torch of freedom.

Opportunities and inventions increased, and exploration expanded as never before. Spiritual and industrial growth in England and America reached unprecedented levels. For both good and bad, revolutionary thinkers arose who pushed the boundaries of every realm. Two philosophers in particular demonstrate the disparity of ideas that arose during this revolutionary period and the effect those differing philosophies had in their application.

Charles-Louis de Secondat, Baron de Montesquieu, a French political philosopher born in 1689, was a prolific author and influential philosopher. His work *The Spirit of the Laws* had great influence in Europe and America. While it was banned by the Catholic Church and received a cold reception throughout France, the American Founders revered Montesquieu's work. His *Spirit of the Laws* was quoted more than any other work during the founding period, second only to the Bible.[36]

"Government should be set up," Montesquieu wrote, "so that no man need be afraid of another."[37] Governmental power originates from the people and must be separated and moderated. Democratic republics require a moral people who carefully guard their liberties and must be led by people with public virtue.

These ideas and others the American Founders studied at length and sought to apply in their new government. Their application of Montesquieu's ideas directly contributed to greater liberty than had hitherto been established anywhere in the world. Montesquieu's words contributed directly to increased freedom and prosperity.

Jean-Jacques Rousseau was a Swiss-born French philosopher, twenty-three years younger than Montesquieu. His ideas differed significantly from Montesquieu's and had widely different results in their application. Rousseau felt that individuals must surrender some of their freedoms to the authority of the state. Human rights, Rousseau stated, did not come from a Creator or from the people but originated from the collective society from which people arose.

Rousseau's ideas directly influenced events leading up to the French Revolution, including increased state control and the use of printed money. Although this is not the first evidence of the Financial Matrix, it is the first clear documentation of his ideas and influence resulting in years of financed wars, fixed wages, and resultant bankruptcy. Ultimately the French government collapsed in anarchy, followed by the "Reign of Terror," during which half a million people were arrested and tens of thousands were executed. Napoleon Bonaparte arose as a dictator, and seventy years of dictatorships ensued.

Rousseau's words became a mighty and powerful sword wielded by tyrants and dictators, resulting in the loss of liberty and life. "Ideas have consequences," wrote Richard M. Weaver,[38] and the consequences of Rousseau's words, and those of others like him, were catastrophic for France and beyond.

Not only were politics influenced by these philosophers; so was religion. Another later Frenchman and philosopher named Alexis de Tocqueville observed the different paths that America and France had taken with regard to religion and politics. In *Democracy in America*, he wrote, "For the Americans the ideas of Christianity and liberty are so completely mingled that it is almost impossible to get them to conceive of one without the other.... In France I had seen the spirits of religion and of freedom almost always marching in opposite directions."

These examples, though limited to two philosophers and two nations, clearly illustrate the cause and effect of leadership and the ideas espoused by nations. On one hand we see leaders who sought to protect people's lives, liberties, and properties; on the other hand we see leaders who sought to oppress through conquering, seizing control of land, and manipulating the monetary system.

The 1700s and 1800s saw revolutions played out again and again in countries throughout the world, all resulting from the ideas of these and other philosophers. Thanks to the works of Montesquieu, John Locke, and Algernon Sydney, the freest, longest-lasting democratic republic in modern time was created in the United States. How many of us today have read their words? How many of us today recognize the cycles of history repeating and know where to turn to learn about what must be done today to preserve our liberties? How many of us see the effects of tyranny today, can speak knowledgeably about the causes that created those circumstances, and know how to reverse them?

Reading about great leaders from history is not enough. By deeply understanding our historical roots, we clearly see the Physical, Land, and Financial Matrices that can smother the torch of freedom. We must be fluent in the ideas of liberty set forth by those before us. Without that understanding we are doomed to repeat the patterns that occurred, leading up to the collapse of all civilizations.

CHAPTER 29

THE ARMED QUAKER

66 Nathanael! Nathanael!"

In response to hearing his name called, the boy with the book, high in the hay loft, attempted to burrow deeper in the straw.

"I know you're up there, Nathanael. You come down right now!" The boy remained quiet. "If you don't come down now, I'm going to light this barn on fire, with your books as fodder!"

The boy's eyes grew wide. "You will not, Jacob Greene! I'm going to tell Ma what you said!" He jumped from the straw and scurried down the ladder, book in tow.

"You go ahead and tell her," his older brother retorted. "She's right ornery since you forgot to bring in the cows last night, and now the garden's ruined!"

Nathanael's face fell. "Oh no! The cows!"

"That's right. If your nose wasn't always stuck in a book, maybe you'd remember to do your chores once in a while!"

"Nathanael!" This time it was Father's voice, and the boy's heart began to pound. He had no fear of being beaten; his father was a Quaker through and through, and violence was not his way.

But with the speech he knew was coming, the young boy almost wished for a beating instead; it would be over sooner and hurt his conscience less.

"Yes, Father," he said meekly.

"Come here, son."

Nathanael approached his father, trying to hide the book behind his back. "Yes, Father?"

"What do we have here?" His father stretched out one hand for the book. For a moment the boy thought he could feign ignorance, but the look in his father's eyes told him otherwise, and he reluctantly handed the book over.

"Nathanael," Father began, "your books are becoming a hindrance to our family, to this farm, and to your own growth." His father's solemn voice filled him with dread. He loved his books; he spent every spare minute reading them and anxiously saved every spare penny for the next volume he hoped to purchase. He'd read every book he owned at least three times, and he loved what he learned from them. But he knew his father's views differed widely from his own. Math, law, politics—his father discouraged his studies, viewing them as a waste of time.

"I'm sorry, Father," he replied. "Please don't take my book! I promise I won't let it happen again. I promise not to cause trouble." His eyes filled with tears, and his father placed a firm hand on his shoulder.

"Nathanael, your help is needed here. We have a busy farm, with many animals and many chores. There's much work to do, and these books have done nothing to help you serve your mother or brother or our community."

The boy's head hung in shame, but he tried once more. "Father, I promise I'll do better. If you have to take my book ever again, then you can have *all* of my books! I promise to do my chores first, and I won't let my reading get in the way of my responsibilities."

Finally his father's face softened, and he handed the book back. "A promise is a solemn thing, son." Nathanael nodded. "I won't forget what you've promised me."

Nathanael's reply came quickly, "Neither will I! And I promise, one day my reading will serve my family and my community. It will, Father!"

His father looked at his son's earnest face and sighed. "We shall see. Come now, Nathanael, let's go explain to Mother what happened with the cows."

Nathanael Greene would indeed grow up to offer great service to not only his family and community but also his nation—not, however, without offering further grief to his father and religious community. Nathanael, determined to be true to his word, took good care of his father's farm and foundry. But much to the consternation of his father and the Quakers, who discouraged intellectual endeavors, he continued to read and study everything he could. Of most particular concern was Nathanael's determination to study military texts.

Nathanael married at age thirty-two, and it was in that same year that relations between the Americans and the British were intensifying. Within months of his marriage, he began to help establish a local militia known as the Kentish Guards. Due to a pronounced limp Nathanael's admittance to the guards was questioned, but he was allowed to participate as a private, the lowest military rank. His admittance, in turn, led to an increased desire to understand military strategy, and so as he had always done, he began to educate himself.

His participation in the militia and militaristic studies, however, did not sit well with Quaker authorities, and his loyalty to the Quaker religion was called into question. Called before a Quaker committee, he insisted he was a Quaker, but that his religion would not keep him from studying and participating in measures to defend his country. In response he was required to quit his membership of the Society of Friends.

Though he held a low rank, Nathanael's capabilities were high, and he quickly worked his way up through the hierarchy. In response to the courage and leadership he demonstrated at the battle of Breed's Hill in Boston, he was promoted to brigadier general. He met General George Washington early in his military career, and the two became fast, lifelong friends. With every task the general gave him, Nathanael excelled, and during the low point of Valley Forge, General Washington entrusted Nathanael with procuring food, clothes, and supplies for the dwindling troops.

Nathanael's dependability and keen strategic bent were demonstrated in a series of tactical achievements that impressed Washington and Congress, and one of Washington's aides reported of him, "He is beyond doubt a first-rate military genius, and one in whose opinions the General places the utmost confidence." This confidence resulted in Washington appointing Nathanael to replace General Horatio Gates when Gates was unable to hold the British on the southern front. Washington was not alone in his desire to place Nathanael in that important position. Alexander Hamilton also told Congress, "For God's sake, let the replacement be Nathanael Greene!"

Nathanael took charge of the south, and though General Cornwallis lost far more men, Nathanael lost both battles of Cowpens and Eutah Springs. After months of evading the superior British troops and another loss at Guildford's courthouse, Nathanael wrote, "I am determined to carry the war into South Carolina."

With the assistance of General Francis Marion (the "Swamp Fox"), Nathanael and his troops began to capture key forts. He avoided pitched battles and relied instead on a strategy of rapid maneuvers that struck at the weakness of British lines, often attacking their points of communication. Though he lost many battles, he won the campaign, eventually forcing Cornwallis to Yorktown for reinforcements. In this way he was influential in bringing about the final scenes of the Revolutionary War.

Nathanael Greene has been memorialized in the names of countless cities, counties, and parks, but though his name has not been erased, the story of his life and sacrifices has begun to fade. His words, however, stand bright as a testament to his contributions as one who boldly passed the flame of liberty on to posterity: "Permit me...to recommend from the sincerity of my heart, ready at all times to bleed in my country's cause, a declaration of independence; and call upon the world, and great God who governs it, to witness the necessity, propriety and rectitude thereof.... Let us, therefore, act like men inspired with a resolution that nothing but the frowns of Heaven shall conquer us."

LESSONS FROM NATHANAEL GREENE ON HOW TO PASS THE TORCH

1. Unlikely beginnings sometimes beget the greatest heroes. Born into humble circumstances, opposed by family and religion, with a physical deformity, Nathanael Greene rose above these circumstances to influence the outcome of a war that would in turn shape the direction of the entire world. His love of God, of liberty, and of country were what mattered most to him and propelled him to persevere despite difficulty.

2. Nathanael's self-education was instrumental in helping him develop into the leader he became (as we see with other historical leaders). Though life didn't offer him an excellent education or easy circumstances, through grit and determination he sought out the education he needed to become one of the nation's most gifted commanders, and his delight in knowledge and his sacrifices to attain an education allowed him to turn the tide of the war and, in doing so, help save the struggling nation.

CHAPTER 30

THE LADY PRESIDENTESS

"Mama, who was the man who came to visit you?"

The young woman blushed and glanced furtively at the older woman in the room, a slave of her former husband. "That was one of Mother's friends, Jacky."

"He's very tall!"

She thought about the dashing visitor, who, at six feet two inches, had towered over her small frame. "Yes, he is, isn't he?"

"I like him!" the young boy announced. "He's very kind. When will he be back, Mama?"

"Why, I don't know." She paused, pondering the same question. Her guest had traveled more than thirty-five miles, one way, to see her that evening, and it was unlikely he would soon make the trip again.

"Why did he come, Mama? Did he want to buy tobacco?"

She laughed. "No, not to buy tobacco…." Her voice trailed off. Why had the gentleman come? It was obvious: he had come to court her, the wealthiest widow in Virginia. But why was she that widow? Why had all this happened to her?

Suddenly tears sprang to her eyes, and she turned from her son so that he would not see them. "Off to bed, Jacky! It's very late. You should have been in bed long ago!" She pushed her protesting son to the arms of his nanny, who carried him away, and then sat at her desk, facing the large mirror it held. "You may go, Eliza," she said to the woman who had been waiting on her, and when the room was empty, she let the tears come. Within seven short years she had gone from the most eligible young woman around, to now Virginia's most eligible widow. How had it happened?

Born into a well-established though by no means wealthy family, she had learned to read and write in an age when most women were illiterate. As did most women of the time, she learned to spin thread, cook, garden, and clean; she learned to weave cloth, sew, and mend.

Only five feet tall, she made up in beauty and charm for what she lacked in stature. When the son of the wealthiest man in Virginia came to court when she was just nineteen, she won over his crusty father and secured a happy marriage to a plantation owner. Together they buried two children, but she never dreamed that after seven short years she would bury her husband as well. And yet that had come to pass. Here she was, only twenty-six years old, and her husband was gone.

She looked in the mirror and wiped away the tears, sitting a little taller as she remembered what came next. The responsibility of running the vast plantations now fell solely on her. Within a month of his passing, she had harvested the tobacco crop on time and had it cured, packed, and shipped to the market. She'd informed her husband's associates of his passing and requested that future correspondence be sent to her. She had capably bargained for the best tobacco prices with London merchants, while continuing to oversee the household and the rearing of her children. She had stepped into her husband's shoes with courage and bravery, but it had been difficult. That had been just a year ago, but a long year it had been.

Her thoughts turned back to that evening's visitor. The young military general had promised to call again, and in her heart she hoped she would see him soon. He was well known for his fairness, bravery, and immense courage, having demonstrated each of those in the conflict between the French and the Indians. He would make a good husband and father, of that much the young woman felt sure.

Within a fortnight General George Washington did call again, and not long after that the couple was betrothed. In December of that same year, Washington resigned his military commission, and in January they were married.

The first years of their marriage were spent at Washington's estate overlooking the Potomac at Mount Vernon. Martha loved her role as housekeeper, wife, and mother; she loved the private, quiet life surrounded by family and close friends. Throughout the time to come, she would look back on those early years of their marriage with longing, wishing to return to that period.

But the serene, agrarian life was not their lot. The start of the Revolutionary War launched the Washingtons into the heart of the conflict and into the center of American society. George Washington left Mount Vernon in 1775, not to return to his beloved home for more than six years while the war raged.

At Washington's request, Martha joined Washington and his troops each winter at their encampments, caring for the general and socializing with the wives of the other officers. She witnessed firsthand the brutal conditions of wartime encampments and occasional conflicts, the ice and snow, the lack of clothing, and the shortage of food.

Every year it got worse. She responded by sending requests to Esther Reed in Philadelphia, and together with Martha Jefferson, Thomas Jefferson's wife, the women organized sewing circles to sew shirts, mend breeches and coats, and knit stockings to clothe the freezing troops. Even the loyalists were pestered for funds to such an extent that they finally contributed, in an effort to get rid of the women.

Martha also visited the wounded soldiers and nursed their injuries. She sought to raise the morale of the troops and keep things as normal as possible by putting on dinner parties and dances. Though surrounded by battlefields and the brutality of war, she brought her gifts of gentility and healing, blessing all with whom she came in contact.

When the war ended and Washington assumed the presidency, her role as First Lady—or as some called her the "Lady Presidentess"[39] thrust her even more fully into the spotlight. Day and night, night and day she entertained and hosted, confiding to a friend once that her role made her feel "more like a state prisoner than anything else." Nevertheless, Martha would say later of those trying times, "I am determined to be cheerful and happy in whatever situation I may find myself. For I have learned that the greater part of misery or unhappiness is determined not by our circumstances but by our disposition."

It was that inner resolve that allowed Martha Washington to bury two husbands and each of her children; that resolve allowed

her to accompany Washington to the battle's edge and preside with
him as host of balls and banquets; and that resolve sustained her in
times of illness and death, in the blossom of youth and the evening
of life. Her disposition eventually propelled and allowed her to
stand by her husband, the first president of a fledgling nation, the
greatest hope for freedom humankind had ever seen.

Martha Washington serves as a reminder to all who would pass
the torch of liberty that both men and women paid a high price for
our nation's birth, and we must not forget their sacrifices and the
lessons their lives share with us.

LESSONS FROM MARTHA WASHINGTON ON HOW TO PASS THE TORCH

1. Perhaps above all else, Martha serves as an example of willingly giving all that is required to the cause of liberty. When her only surviving son begged to join Washington in the conflict, she let him go, well knowing the price of his service could be his life. When he died, she did not resent the war or her son's choice to serve but knew that liberty is a costly endeavor and that she and her husband had given all they could to ensuring its protection and perpetuation.

2. Martha's grace, courage, and determination serve as an example that though the ongoing fight for freedom is strung with thorns and difficulties, the softening influence of women and family can serve to strengthen and remind everyone of the beauties of life, even in the midst of hardship. In 1773 one Virginian wrote, "If Men did not converse with Women, [men] would be less perfect and happy than they are."[40] Martha's life was an example of conversing with and serving with generosity and care the soldier, statesman, and commoner.

CHAPTER 31

THE ORPHAN STATESMAN

"**N**o, no, *no*, my friend!" The young man pounded his fist on the table, and the man he spoke to let out a laugh that shook his entire frame. "You've got it all wrong, all wrong, I say!"

"And *you*," retorted his companion, "have got it all right, I presume?"

Frederic smiled broadly. "That I have, and I shall convince you of such, I swear it!"

His friend, Felix, let out another laugh and then replied, "Perhaps you shall, but don't be so sure. Look what Rousseau says here." A common text lay before the two young men, and Felix pointed to passage as he read aloud: "The right which each individual has to his own estate is always subordinate to the right which the community has over all: without this, there would be neither stability in the social tie, nor real force in the exercise of Sovereignty."[41]

Frederic smiled broadly, "But Rousseau, dear Felix, was wrong! Rousseau was convinced that society is a human contrivance. The distance between the lawgiver and the rest of mankind, according to Rousseau, is vast."

Frederic swiftly crossed the room to the window and pointed to a plow in the fields below. "According to Rousseau, the gulf between lawgiver and mankind is the same as that which separates the inventor of that plow from the inert matter of which it is composed."

Felix listened intently. Even if he disagreed with his friend, he had to admit Frederic's reasoning was sound.

Frederic continued, "In Rousseau's opinion, the law should transform persons and should create—or not create—property. But in my opinion, society, persons, property…why, these exist *prior* to law! Property does not exist because there are laws, Felix, but laws exist because there is property. And *property exists because of man's labor.*" His index finger was pointed toward the sky, and he emphasized these last words with a firm, repeated shake of his hand.

Felix pondered Frederic's words and then answered him. "But Rousseau is far from the only proponent of this idea, Frederic! Many others agree that property belongs to society and is subject to it."

"True, true, and where did Rousseau's ideas come from? Where did Robespierre's? Louis Blanc's?" His voice rose. "The Romans, I tell you! From the Romans down to us, through the teaching of law, classical studies, the political theorists of the eighteenth century—on down through the revolutionaries of 1793 and now the modern proponents of a planned social order. But they are all wrong! The rights to property, Felix, are a result of a worker's *labor*, not a legislator's law."

Felix smiled reluctantly. "Well, perhaps you are right after all, but you seem to be alone in your views."

"That may be the case," replied his friend, "But I shan't be for long. I intend to educate the people about the law and about property. It is fundamental, and a good economist knows it's not enough for legislators to know these things."

Felix patted his friend on the back, "If anyone can do it, you can, my friend. Frederic Bastiat, esteemed economist, legislator, and statesman! I can see it now!"[42] The men laughed and returned to their studies, and that budding youth made good on his promise.

Frederic Bastiat was born in 1801 in a port town on the Bay of Biscay in France. His father, an established businessman, moved from the seaside town to an inland estate acquired after the French Revolution when his wife, Frederic's mother, suddenly passed away. Only three years later his father also passed away, and Frederic was left in his grandfather's care. Frederic was an astute student, but by age seventeen he left his formal education to work in his uncle's export business, where Bastiat's father had once been a partner.

As an exporter, Bastiat saw firsthand the evils of protectionism, which flow from financial manipulation. All around, he saw the impact of trade restrictions: warehouses no longer in business, empty homes, deepening poverty, and lines of unemployed men and women. These circumstances troubled Bastiat, and for the next twenty years he dedicated himself to formal and informal economic study. After six years at his uncle's side, he returned to the family estate in Mugron. There he began taking care of his ailing grandfather, but his grandfather soon passed away. This left Bastiat, aged twenty-four, sole executor of the family estate.

Surrounded by fertile fields and a large library, Bastiat hired laborers to work the family farm and he and his friend, Felix Coudroy, began the next important part of Bastiat's education. Together the friends read voraciously and discussed works on philosophy, religion, and poetry; works on politics, history, and travel. This reading, discussion, and debate shaped Bastiat's perspectives on law and government, and it was in these conversations that he formed an understanding of economic principles that he would teach and advocate for the remainder of his life.

In these library discussions, Bastiat converted Felix to classical liberalism, away from Rousseau's socialism. Using that same reasoning, Bastiat later wrote a series of essays and books that came to have worldwide impact.

France's 1830 middle-class revolution spurred Bastiat to become politically active. He was first elected justice of the peace in 1831, and in 1848 he was elected to the national legislative assembly. Leading up to his time in the legislature, he began to publish manuscripts on economics, focusing on the impact of French and English tariffs. A manuscript of his published in 1844 became the most persuasive argument for free trade ever published in France and possibly throughout all of Europe.

His simple, well-reasoned articles garnered him national and international fame, and through his influence all trade restrictions were abolished in England by 1850, and almost all of France's trade restrictions were abolished ten years later, after Bastiat's death. At the same time, free-trade associations inspired by his works sprang up throughout Europe in Belgium, Italy, Sweden, Prussia, and Germany.

Bastiat once warned, "I believe we are entering on a path in which plunder, under very gentle, very subtle, very ingenious forms, embellished with the beautiful names of solidarity and fraternity, is going to assume proportions the extent of which the imagination hardly dares to measure."

It's not enough to know about Bastiat and his influence. The perpetuation and protection of liberty require that each new generation understands the idea themselves that Bastiat wrote of. Without such an understanding, we are doomed to repeat the cycles of bondage and tyranny that have ever followed the path of the unlearned.

LESSONS FROM FREDERIC BASTIAT ON HOW TO PASS THE TORCH

1. The basics of a great education are simple: reading, writing, discussing, year after year after year. Bastiat spent decades immersed in great works, accompanied with experiences that shaped his perspective and desire to expand people's liberty and happiness. Without that time immersed in the greatest ideas of all time, it's likely Bastiat's own ideas would never have become the classics they are today, and his influence would not have been as great as it in fact remains.

2. At the same time that Bastiat wrote *The Law* and other key works, Marx was composing *Das Kapital*, a key text of communism. These two texts, diametrically opposed, are each an example of the power of an idea to shape a nation and world and the importance of understanding human nature in applying economic and political principles. Bastiat's works demonstrate a realistic understanding of human nature, whereas Marx's works presume human motives that are unlikely and unprecedented. Bastiat's deep understanding of divine law and classical truths allowed him to see beyond what it seen to what is unseen and to reveal that vision to the world.

CHAPTER 32

THE UNSCHOOLED SCHOLAR

A boy, short and unkempt, sat with a grunt on an alleyway step. He opened a well-worn book and began examining its contents. Each page was illustrated with hand-drawn flowers, animals, and motifs. He had drawn the figures himself, and he had plans to similarly illustrate his next volume, *The History of Peppin*.

The trouble was, the book cost four pennies, and he had only three. He had unsuccessfully spent the day trying to earn the final coin, and his disappointment was acute. How long would he have to wait for his next book?

"Hello, John!" his cousin's voice rang out cheerily.

"Hello, Samuel." He sighed.

His cousin tossed something in the air and caught it again, and as he did so the sparkle of a coin revealed itself to John.

"Have you a penny?" John asked anxiously.

"I have!" Samuel was exultant. "And I know exactly what I shall do with it! I shall buy a book!"

John was crestfallen, but a sudden thought lit his eyes. "What kind of book, Samuel? One for pictures or for the story?"

His cousin looked at him suspiciously. "For story. But what do you care?"

"Oh, no reason," John replied slyly. "But if you were to give me your penny, I would promise you in return a much larger, better story than any you could purchase for that sum. What's more, I'll paint you a picture at the beginning as well. There are no pictures in penny books, you know...."

The young cousin thought on John's words and then announced, "You shall have the penny!" He tossed John the coin and then sat at his cousin's side.

For the next hour Samuel quietly watched John perform his work, and when the story and illustration were complete, he affirmed that his penny had been well spent. John, with even greater satisfaction, took the penny and ran to purchase his book.

A few months later the same young bibliophile found himself prostrate and unwell. He felt awful, and he could not remember how he came to be in this particular room or bed. He could remember a book had been promised him by a neighbor, however, and he wanted desperately to know its whereabouts.

Day after day a blinding headache plagued him, making it impossible to think or even speak clearly. Gradually it diminished, and as it did, his interest in the book increased. One day when he was more alert than usual, a small group had gathered in his room, including his mother, aunt, and cousins. With great earnestness he asked his mother for the book and was deeply puzzled by her reply. Her lips moved, but made no noise; her hands waved about as if trying to communicate something.

"Why do you not speak?" he cried at last, "Pray, let me have the book!"

His mother and aunt seemed troubled, and then finally his cousin left the room. He returned with a slate, which he handed to John. "The neighbor has reclaimed his book; you are too weak to read," the slate read.

"But why do you write to me?" John exclaimed. "Why not speak? Speak! Speak!"

All exchanged troubled looks, and then his mother, with trembling hand, wrote on the slate and handed it to him with tears in her eyes: "YOU ARE DEAF."[43]

John Kitto later learned he had fallen from a roof to the cobblestone street below. He had been helping his father, a mason, on a roofing project, and whether due to anxiety over a book or excitement about a new shirt his grandmother had promised, he could not later recall. Whatever the cause, he had tripped, and the results were disastrous.

He had lain unconscious for a week, and then for four months more he lay almost immobile and senseless. Gradually he regained consciousness and memory, but he was profoundly, completely deaf. Kitto's family could scarcely afford to feed a growing youth with a large appetite and no ability to contribute to the needs of the family, and so his alcoholic father and overworked mother turned him out of their home when it became clear he would never fully recover.

Kitto barely supported himself for a while by fetching odd pieces of rope and iron from a local pond, and by painting and selling simple pictures. During that time he was indentured to a master so cruel that he twice attempted suicide, and only when a local dentist took pity on him and offered him an apprenticeship did things take a turn for the better. He served an eighteen-month mission to Malta, and upon his return the dentist who had helped

him before enlisted him as a tutor of his young sons as they jour-
neyed to Baghdad.

As sometimes happens, Kitto's deafness led to greater development of his other senses, and the sights and smells of the foreign
country made a lasting impression on him. He carefully recorded
details of the topography, animals, and architecture of the places he
visited. He documented the agricultural methods and the customs
and habits of the people he observed. On his return to England,
he began to publish illustrated biblical stories, and when a London
publisher named Charles Knight discovered Kitto's talent, he
helped him publish a Penny Cyclopedia that would be read by
millions in Britain and be reprinted in America and beyond.

From a humble worker he became the most significant contrib-
utor to Christian scholarship, writing more than twenty-three books,
including an eight-volume work, *Daily Bible Illustrations*, which he
dedicated to the queen. Of the same work, Charles Spurgeon would
say he found it "to be more interesting than any novel that was ever
written, and as instructive as the heaviest theology."

Kitto overcame incredible odds and developed his native interests and skills to such an extent that his name became known
around the world. Of his life experiences he once wrote, "I perhaps
have as much right as any man that lives, to bear witness that there
is no one so low but that he may rise, no condition so cast down
as to be really hopeless, and no privation which need, of itself, shut
out any man from the paths of honorable exertion or from the
hope of usefulness in life. I have sometimes thought that it was
possibly my mission to affirm and establish these great truths."

Torchbearers like Kitto remind us that individual challenges
and difficulties may in fact serve as a doorway to greatness. Kitto's

example of determination and industry truly illustrate that no circumstances can overwhelm the individual who chooses to rise above them and that each person, regardless of background, position, or physical difficulties, has something to share with others that can lift and ennoble humankind.

LESSONS FROM JOHN KITTO ON HOW TO PASS THE TORCH

1. There are no excuses for failure and no easy paths to greatness. Kitto had virtually no formal schooling and was born into poverty. His grandfather, father, and grandmother all struggled with alcoholism, and as a result he experienced neglect and at times abuse. He was short of stature, deaf, and unwell, experiencing severe headaches throughout his life. Though he experienced deep lows, he ultimately rose above each of the challenges he faced. He used the interests he'd been given, a love of literature and beauty, to bring joy to himself and bless those around him.

2. Our fortunes may change when we least expect it. It's wise not to give up hope when in the midst of difficulty, for sometimes in that difficulty we find inner strengths and talents that would otherwise remain unknown to us. The difficulties of Kitto's life helped illuminate his gifts, and by relying on those gifts, he turned hardship into a heritage of determination and grit.

CHAPTER 33

THE PRINCE OF PREACHERS

The elderly man lay still in his bed, making no sound, his chest barely rising and falling. "Grandfather?" The young woman at his bedside spoke softly. He looked worse than yesterday, she thought with sorrow.

At the sound of her voice his eyes fluttered open. "Sophia!" He reached a trembling hand toward her. "How good to see you! Why did you wait so long to come?"

"I was here yesterday, don't you remember?" She already knew the answer. His memory seemed to be fading as quickly as his body, and the thought saddened her.

She changed the subject. "You wouldn't believe the streets, Grandfather! They say there are over a hundred thousand people gathered today for the preacher's burial!"

Her grandfather looked towards the window. "A hundred thousand? Why, I believe there will be twice that many!"

The girl laughed, "Oh, do you?"

Suddenly the elderly man was serious. "Did I ever tell you the story…?" He paused, searching the recesses of his memory. At these words the girl suppressed a grin. Grandfather was always telling the same stories over and over. She did not doubt she had often heard the one he was about to share.

"Which story, Grandfather?" she asked. "Tell me!"

He looked again toward the window and then began his tale. "It was 1856—no, 1858." He gazed into the distance, struggling to recall the details. "I can't remember. It was long before you were born," he said with a laugh, "but I do remember Fast Day was approaching, and the great preacher was to speak in the Crystal Palace. The Palace was only four or five years old at the time. It was built for the Great Exhibition...."

Grandfather's story was beginning to wander, but the girl didn't mind. The thought of a new story excited her, and she listened closely.

"I still remember the glass walls and ceilings.... My, what a magnificent structure! As I was saying, the preacher was coming to the Crystal Palace. There were to be over twenty-two thousand in attendance! Some of the benches were broken, so they called me in to fix them a day or two before the event.

"I was there alone, working on the benches high in the gallery, when I heard it. I still remember the words with perfect clarity. 'Behold the Lamb of God, which taketh away the sin of the world.'"

His eyes clouded over, and tears spilled from them. "It was an angel, I was sure, speaking to me. Oh, my child, how those words pierced my soul. Never before had I felt so troubled by my sins, nor so much hope that perhaps I could change. I left my tools then and there—they fetched old Charlie to bring them to me the next day." He chuckled "I went straight home. For days I prayed, struggling for my soul. And I saw Him, Annie! I saw Him!"

His granddaughter looked in astonishment. "You saw *who*, Grandfather?"

His voice was full of emotion when he replied, "The good Lord, Annie. He brought me peace, and ever since I have tried to live according to His ways. Yes, I have that preacher to thank for saving my soul and turning me to God!"

Annie looked in confusion at her grandfather. "But what does that preacher have to do with it?"

He lifted a finger and pointed at her as he responded gravely, "It was his voice I heard that morning! I later learned he had gone to the Palace to determine the position of the platform for his speech the next day. He wished to test the acoustics of that building, and it was he who cried out that morning. I didn't know he was there, but his words stirred my soul and brought me to the Lord. It was that Charles Spurgeon, the Prince of Preachers they call him, whose words touched my soul."

That man's life was one of hundreds of thousands to be touched throughout the world by the great preacher, Charles Spurgeon. Spurgeon lived during a period of great opportunity in England and beyond. Exploration throughout the world was at a high point, and religious and political liberty were expanding along with that exploration. During his lifetime England saw the end of slavery (something Spurgeon himself promoted, despite falling into disfavor for doing so), and that country also experienced unprecedented spiritual and industrial growth during his life.

Spurgeon was born in a small community in Essex, and his fondest, earliest memories were of looking at the pictures in *Pilgrim's Progress* and *Foxe's Book of Martyrs*. Though his formal schooling was limited, he loved reading, and his library eventually grew to over twelve thousand volumes.

When but fifteen years old Spurgeon had a conversion experience, and shortly after that he began working as a Sunday school teacher. When a friend could not make a commitment to give a sermon in a Teversham cottage, Spurgeon was asked to step in. He spent what little time he had preparing word-for-word what he would say and then laid it aside as he gave his first public sermon. Those how heard him speak were enthralled by his abilities, and the teenage-preacher's popularity quickly grew.

Before his twentieth birthday he was invited to be pastor over the largest congregation in London, the famed New Park Street Chapel. Before he was appointed, attendance at the church had begun to dwindle, but following his appointment the attendance grew and grew until a new building, and then another and another, were required to hold the Sabbath gatherings. Ultimately his congregation moved to the Metropolitan Tabernacle, which held a congregation of fifty-six hundred.

By age twenty-two, Spurgeon was the most popular preacher of his day. Not everyone admired his liberal theology and strict piety, but throughout the world copies of his speeches were translated and spread, and every week his Sunday sermons were distributed to devout Christians who found in his words an incomparable explanation of what it meant to be a Christian and a clear defense of the truths they held dear.

David Livingstone carried a copy of Spurgeon's sermons with him in his travels. On the first page of a text he carried with him he wrote, "Very good. D.L.," and after his death that copy was returned to Spurgeon, who counted it among his greatest possessions. Ever a defender of gospel truths, he despised "progress" at the expense of principle, calling it "progress from the truth, which being interpreted, is progressing backwards."

Spurgeon served as pastor of the New Park Street Chapel for more than thirty-eight years; he started orphanages and charities and a college that was later named after him. His published works include sermons, an autobiography, commentaries, books of prayer, devotionals, magazines, and hymns. He died at age fifty-seven, but his legacy lives on as one of the greatest preachers of all time.

Pastor Spurgeon sits at the top of a great list of men and women of history who not only impacted their own time for good but also left a lasting contribution for which the world is indebted.

LESSONS FROM CHARLES SPURGEON ON HOW TO PASS THE TORCH

1. Spurgeon stands as an example that being well read is not enough to have lasting influence. It's also important to be versed in current events and to connect with one's audience in meaningful ways. Spurgeon's influence rested, in large part, on his great gifts of communication. He had an interest in the day's happenings; he knew about the events of his time and what concerns and challenges faced his congregations. He knew what was going on at home and abroad. He studied contemporaries and those who came before. This allowed him to connect and identify with his hearers, and as he spoke passionately, his message resonated with those who heard him.

2. Spurgeon felt led and inspired of God; this enabled him to preach in a way that stirred and moved his listeners to action. Though some criticized, most admired his sincerity and knowledge. This sincerity aided him in advocating unpopular topics (such as antislavery measures). Spurgeon relied on the Lord, saying, "Let each man find out what God wants him to do, and then let him do it, or die in the attempt." He practiced what he preached, and his influence increased because of the integrity he demonstrated.

CHAPTER 34

THE BELL-RINGER OF THE COMMON PEOPLE

"**B**ram, what's wrong?" Her usually outspoken husband had returned home without a word and sat at the table in silence. Though they had been married only a short time, Johanna knew her husband well enough to discern that something was clearly amiss. "Bram?" she called him again.

"The strangest thing just happened," he remarked, as much to himself as to her. "I've been visiting my parishioners in their homes, as you know." She nodded in response. "Being new here, I have hoped to get to know them and learn their views. I just met a peasant woman in the street, Pietronella Baltus." He gave his wife a searching look. "Have you met her?"

She shook her head. "No, I haven't."

"She refused to shake my hand," he said, puzzlement etching his brow.

"But why?" asked his wife, surprised that any person would find her husband so objectionable.

"She seems to despise me!" he exclaimed. "At last I prevailed upon her, and she relented, but she told me clearly she would shake my hand only because I am a fellow human being and not because I am her brother in Christ. Further, she did not hesitate to inform me my soul is in danger of hellfire...."

Johanna stared in confusion at her husband. "What could induce her to say such a thing?"

Bram shook his head and muttered, "I suppose she disagrees with my religious views. But I intend to find out more. I shall visit her again tomorrow."

"Visit her again...tomorrow? Don't you think it's better to leave her be for now? She doesn't sound very interested in you or your new position. And she certainly doesn't think much of the state of your soul!"

Bram continued to stew, and seemed not to hear his wife's words. "My pride has been bruised, that is a fact, but when was tarnished pride ever something that stopped a servant of Christ? I think it should rather propel me to greater discipleship. Perhaps I have something to teach her, and if not, then she most certainly has something to teach me."

Johanna shook her head. "Once you're determined to do something, I know there's no stopping you, but please, wait a day or two before visiting her again. What good can come of it?"

Bram couldn't answer, but good or bad, he felt something would come from learning about that woman's bold declarations.

True to his word, he returned to Pietronella's home and then returned again and again. Many of the villagers in Beesd, where Bram had been called, were modern and worldly. But Pietronella represented a different class. Her home was humble and obscure, and her views were far from worldly. He was preaching false doctrine, she told him, and unless he changed his views, he might sooner hope to sprout wings than enter heaven.

Slowly the words of Pietronella and other humble villagers worked on Bram's soul. Slowly his perspective of religion and the "Reformed fathers" shifted away from liberal modernism toward the Reformed churches. He turned to the scriptures as he never had before, and as he did so, he experienced a mighty transformation. Little did he know his transformation would set the stage for a lifetime of mighty contributions to religion and politics, stretching from the Netherlands to distant parts of the world.

Abraham Kuyper, or "Bram" as his family called him, was born in a small seaside village of Maassluis in the Netherlands. The Reformed churches of the Netherlands had, over time, become apostate. "Modernists" held political, academic, and religious positions, and the church was led by people who spent little time in the scriptures and much time seeking the things of the world.

Kuyper, educated first at home under the tutelage of his mother and then in a public secondary school, excelled in linguistics and many other subjects. He graduated from the University of Leiden with high honors and by the age of twenty-six had earned a PhD in theology. Along with his academic talents he was also a gifted organizer, and he was drawn to movements and organizations, where he found a natural place at the head.

After preaching in Beesd, Kuyper moved next to Utrecht, with a congregation of thirty-five thousand members and eleven ministers, and then to Amsterdam where the church had one hundred forty thousand members and twenty-eight ministers. Whenever and wherever he preached, throngs gathered. His oratory was powerful, as was his command of various languages. What was more, he had a gift for stirring the souls of his listeners, and those who heard his sermons long remembered his words and the feelings they evoked.

His influence was not limited to religion. He helped make popular the Anti-Revolutionary Party and served as its undisputed leader for over forty years. Later in life he served as Dutch prime minister from 1901 to 1905. Throughout his life he advocated the idea of "Sphere Sovereignty." God, he believed, had created institutions or spheres (including church, family, education, and state). Each sphere was sovereign in its own right and, he believed, governed by what he called ordinances or rules set forth by God. Whenever any one sphere grew too powerful or centralized, bondage resulted. But when the spheres were balanced and equally powerful, freedom ensued.

In addition to politics and religion, Abraham Kuyper excelled as a journalist, writing on both religious and political subjects, even starting his own newspaper. He also opened the Free University in Amsterdam and served as professor of theology there.

Some of Kuyper's greatest contributions resulted from the efforts he made to defend religious liberty and provide equal protection for all religions. He was a champion of faith-based organizations such as schools, newspapers, hospitals, and youth movements, and he sought for equal government treatment and support of such institutions. A defender of the poor and humble, he was known as the "bell-ringer of the common people," for though he had great influence and power, his interest was in helping simple folk.

In a time when people were apathetic or even hostile to religion, Kuyper argued persuasively in its defense. His name is on a list of many torchbearers who have been erased and nearly forgotten by modern historicists. It is our duty today to recognize that history provides many examples of people standing up against tyranny and defending liberty. Kuyper is one statesman who did so and who should always be remembered for his impact and efforts.

LESSONS FROM ABRAHAM KUYPER ON HOW TO PASS THE TORCH

1. We learn from Kuyper's life that there is not one specific path by which to influence history or one specific method for becoming an influential leader. Kuyper combined religion and politics in a rare way. He successfully championed greater political liberty and religious freedom and protection through his efforts, thereby influencing the direction of his country through both political and religious means.

2. Kuyper's ideas help illustrate the original intention of the idea of "separation of church and state" and show how religions and government can work together for the good of the whole. The spheres of influence that Kuyper extolled demonstrate that family, religion, government, and education are all key elements of society that must be both limited and empowered to act in their distinct areas. When any one element gains too much control, liberty is lost, and religious worship always suffers as a result.

CHAPTER 35

THE "SHRIMP" WHO STOPPED SLAVERY

I t was late afternoon on a brilliant spring day in May and growing uncomfortably warm. Three young men were gathered on a
knoll under the sprawling branches of a massive oak tree, enjoying its shade. They had spent a lively afternoon discussing a variety
of subjects, as was their habit.

They had much in common. Each of them, born within six
months of each other, was twenty-six; each was named William,
and each had begun a promising political career at a young age.
The first, William Pitt, was serving as the prime minister of Britain,
the youngest prime minister of that country ever elected. The
second, William Grenville, was serving as a member of Parliament
and Paymaster of the Forces. The last, William Wilberforce, was
serving as a member of Parliament representing Yorkshire, one of
the most powerful seats in the House of Commons.

Naturally their conversation had a political bent, and as the
afternoon wore on, their discussions turned to a topic that was on
each of their minds.

"Wilberforce, you ought to do it. Do it before someone else does!" Grenville leaned with his back against the tree and tossed a pebble toward his friend as he spoke. Wilberforce caught the pebble and began to examine it casually.

"I second that," Pitt chimed in. "Why don't you give notice of a motion on the subject of the slave trade? You have already taken great pains to collect evidence, and are therefore fully entitled to the credit which doing so will ensure you. Do not lose time, or the ground will be occupied by another!"

Wilberforce didn't answer, but continued to examine the pebble.

Grenville spoke again: "Clarkson's been meeting with you every week, has he not?" Wilberforce nodded in response. "For what, three months now? You've told me yourself you have a table full of firsthand evidence on the evils of the slave trade. And you know the Quakers will provide whatever you might lack, if more evidence is needed!"

Wilberforce listened thoughtfully. "There are more respected, more capable members than I," he countered.

"None more witty!" Grenville remarked, and the group laughed.

"If the slaves are to be saved by wit, heaven help us!" Wilberforce countered.

"You have some other virtues," Pitt laughed. "Why, didn't the Prince of Wales say he would go anywhere in the world to hear you sing?"

Wilberforce grimaced. "So I am to become a singing MP and by my dulcet tunes sway all of Britain, the world's most powerful country, to abandon her most lucrative trade?"

Grenville's laughing increased. "Hear, hear!" he cried. "And so you shall! Did not Boswell, after hearing you speak, write about 'the mere shrimp that mounted on the table, and grew and grew until it became a whale,' so persuasive was your speech?"

Wilberforce took careful aim, throwing the pebble back at his friend forcefully. "The 'singing shrimp of York'…I can picture it now! And thank you very much for the reminder. I had hoped to forget that sweet commentary on my abilities!"

More laughter ensued, then Pitt replied in a more serious tone, "Wilberforce, you have more natural eloquence than the of us combined. Use it for this!"

The young man looked at the wide expanse of green around them. He realized he had years ago made his choice to defend the slaves, when he had converted to Christianity. Since his conversion, over the course of time, his path had become clear to him. His cause was the cause of humankind. God, it seemed, had at this time set the way before him to use his abilities to abolish the slave trade.

"I shall," he responded simply. "I must." In later years, William Wilberforce avowed he could still "distinctly remember the very knoll on which I was sitting near Pitt and Grenville" where that fateful decision was pronounced.[44]

For forty years Wilberforce fought against the slave trade, and just three days before his death a bill outlawing the slave trade in most of the British colonies was finally passed. It had been the battle of a lifetime, and he felt it deserved everything he could give to the cause.

Born into the upper middle class, William Wilberforce demonstrated an academic bent early on. Though he was small, sickly, and plagued by eye problems, with a back bent out of shape, the unassuming Wilberforce commanded a mighty presence when he began to speak. He secured a seat in the House of Commons just after his twenty-first birthday, and within two years he had ascended to the premiership. Six months after that he stood for one of the most powerful seats in the House of Commons, representing Yorkshire, and won. Soon after that he began to travel abroad, and discussions with a traveling companion sparked within him a change of heart and direction that would shape the course of Wilberforce's life.

He described this conversion as a "great change," and though outwardly he remained his happy, witty, brilliant self, inwardly he struggled deeply over personal weaknesses. At first uncertain whether the life of a politician could blend with his newfound faith, he was finally convinced by Pitt and other friends, including John Newton, that not only could his faith allow him to continue in politics, it could shape and magnify his influence there.

With that new courage and conviction, Wilberforce's trajectory remained political, but his interests and efforts expanded a hundredfold. He helped found a colony in Sierra Leone for freed slaves; he established a society for the prevention of animal abuse; from hospitals for the poor to a national art gallery, from an institution dedicated to scientific research to public health initiatives and prison reform, from instituting shorter working hours to improving factory conditions, from England to Africa and beyond, Wilberforce's influence was immense.

He personally led or belonged to sixty-nine different benevolent societies, working with Christians, atheists, Muslims, Buddhists, and all who would join him in his cause to benefit humanity. From king to slave, president to servant, in England and beyond, Wilberforce's efforts and interest touched the world.

He composed a *Practical View of Real Christianity*, which became a best-selling book during his time, pleading with Britons to apply true Christian principles in their lives and to their hearts. Though plagued by pleurisy throughout his life, he was never distracted from his forty-year crusade to free the slaves and eliminate Europe's largest economic industry. Through bridge-building and determination, Wilberforce and his friends attacked a seemingly insurmountable evil and won.

Before his death one biographer says Wilberforce asked his best friend and colleague, Henry Thornton, "Well, Henry, what shall we abolish next?" Let us ask the same question: What shall we abolish next?—and strive to live with the same compassion, determination, and conviction as did one of the greatest reformers the world has ever known.

LESSONS FROM WILLIAM WILBERFORCE ON HOW TO PASS THE TORCH

1. Unquestionably much of what Wilberforce accomplished could never have been done by an unaided individual. The issues he tackled were too immense, the lives at stake too many. Wilberforce teaches us that groups united passionately together for a common, moral cause can have immense impact. Community building and networking have a powerful ability to shape the course of history. Those who would pass the torch of freedom today must unite with others, both those similar and dissimilar, around a common goal, combining their efforts for the larger good.

2. Those who impact the world for the better come in many shapes and sizes and from a variety of backgrounds. Many of us have the false notion that a leader must be of a certain physical stature, outspoken, and charismatic. This simply is not true. William Wilberforce was slight of build and walked hunched over from a dowager's hump; he was sickly and physically unimpressive. Despite those features, he made a great impact for good. What matters most is the strength of our conviction and our loyalty to God and the causes placed in our path.

CHAPTER 36

THE BLACK MOSES

"**M**uthuh, what do ya reckon them ships be doin'?"

The black woman looked up from her task. Two ships, much larger than those that usually came this way, were slowly making their way up the Combahee River. They were too far away to discern details, but word had spread that a Confederate–Union combat was likely, and she certainly didn't want to be caught in the middle of it.

"Looks like trouble," she said slowly, glancing anxiously toward the slave quarters, more than a quarter-mile away.

"Should we go?" asked her son. They looked around the field and saw worried looks on the faces of the other slaves. Shouts arose in the distance, and the woman anxiously grabbed her son's hand.

"Leave the cotton!" she yelled at him as he struggled to pull the full bag behind them. They began to run toward the slave quarters as panic spread across the fields. Her concern grew as she noticed smoke coming from the direction of their living quarters.

Then they heard shooting in the distance, heavy artillery fire, and the woman began to pray aloud as she ran. "Please, Lord, keep my babies safe! Good Lord, protect us!" Her son ran ahead of her and reached the quarters before she did. Shouts and cries filled the air, chickens squawking, men yelling, babies crying, and in the chaos she called out frantically for her children. "Charles! Eliza! Samuel!"

With relief she saw Charles running toward her with baby Samuel in his arms and Eliza following close behind as fast as her short legs could carry her.

"Union ships, Muthuh! *Union!*" Charles called out, but the words made no sense to her. "They be Union troops, and the Confederate forces be comin'!"

The woman looked around and noticed the slaves running, en masse, to the ships and slowly realization dawned on her. "We be free!" she cried out with glee, "we be free!"

Her son's face showed no such happiness. "Not yet, Muthuh! Run! Run!"

They turned back to the fields and ran through them pell-mell toward the river, on and on through the fields. Little Eliza fell and let out a cry. The woman snatched her up and continued running, her lungs burning and her legs on fire but a smile on her face. *Freedom!* she thought over and over. Overseers began to chase the slaves; one stepped in front of her, demanding she turn around, but the ship was well within sight now, and she had no intention of listening to him. She dodged his swinging arms and ran with greater urgency toward the ships.

When they reached the bank's edge, they found it overflowing with slaves. Hundreds of them lined the water, and smaller boats from the larger ships were waiting to pick them up.

"Lookee there!" exclaimed the mother as she saw a young girl with two pigs making her way to the boats.

"Me and the pigs, *both*!" the girl exclaimed, and the soldiers, laughing, welcomed her aboard. Soon the small boats were beyond full, but they were prevented from returning to the larger ship by the waiting throngs.

"Don't leave us!" —"Take me! Take me!"

Oarsmen beat them back, but the slaves would not let go until it became clear the boats would only return when all 750 of them were safe on board.

"Freedom! Freedom!" The woman continued crying to herself. It was too wonderful to believe. When she finally stepped aboard the ship, she openly wept. Though the scene was utter chaos, women with pails of food on their heads, children hanging from mothers' necks, pigs running and chickens squawking, she had never been so happy in her life. She hugged her small brood and then stood to thank the soldiers.

"Don't thank me," said one young gunman. "Thank Miz Tubman yonder. This was her idea!"

The woman he pointed to was barely five feet tall, her dress in tatters from the rush of slaves who had clambered aboard the ship and clung to her for help. Miz Tubman noticed the woman staring at her, and approached her.

"Is it true you thunk this all up, Miz Tubman?" asked the woman, tears pouring down her cheeks.

"Yes, ma'am," she answered. "Call me Minty, please. And welcome to freedom."

Harriet Tubman was born a slave and so was subjected from her youth to regular lashings and abuse. When she was a youth, an overseer struck her unconscious with a two-pound weight aimed at the head. She lay unresponsive for some time, and when she revived, she was sent directly to the fields to work, blood pouring from her wound.

She attempted to do as commanded, but seizures, a result of her injury which remained throughout her life, prohibited her from working profitably in the field. Blackouts and debilitating headaches also plagued her, and she knew her usefulness as a slave was limited. She worried about what would happen to her now that she was no longer seen as a contributing slave. When her owner died, she decided to attempt an escape, and in 1849 she successfully found her way to Pennsylvania, a state where slavery was outlawed.

Once she realized she was on free soil, she said, she looked down at her hands to see if she was still the same person. "There was such a glory over everything," she explained; "the sun came like gold through the trees, and over the fields, and I felt like I was in Heaven."[45] Freedom was indeed sweet, but not half as sweet alone as it would be with family and friends. Over the remaining years of her life Harriet returned again and again into the slave states, nineteen times in all, risking her life to bring to freedom her family and all those who were willing to make the dangerous trek.

Harriet became a key figure in the Underground Railroad, a network of antislavery connections that led escapees from slave states to the free north. Through her efforts she guided her parents, most of her siblings, and more than three hundred slaves in total to freedom. In leading the raid on the Combahee River, she became the first woman to lead an armed expedition during the war, and in doing so was instrumental in freeing an additional seven hundred–plus slaves.

That raid was so successful that other raids were later patterned after it, and Harriet was heard to say her only regret that day was the choice of her dress, which was ruined by slaves clamoring for her help aboard the boat she was on. Because of her role in bringing slaves from bondage to freedom, she was called the Black Moses, and people such as Frederick Douglass and John Brown counted her among the South's greatest heroes and emancipators.

Today Harriet Tubman has been called a symbol of the "enduring spirit of this nation." She explained, "I always tol' God, 'I'm goin' to hol' steady on you, an' you've got to see me through.'"

Her example of "holding steady" and risking her life time after time truly makes her one of the greatest underground historical leaders who ever carried the torch of freedom.

LESSONS FROM HARRIET TUBMAN ON HOW TO PASS THE TORCH

1. The slavery that Harriet Tubman knew was eventually outlawed, but there is still a great need today for emancipators of all kinds, from financial to political, from sex trafficking to forced labor. Harriet's life teaches us that emancipation from bondage requires concerted effort and is not the work of any one generation but the task of all defenders of liberty, throughout all time. While slavery has been present in all civilizations to varying degrees, Harriet Tubman reminds us that every human soul yearns for liberty, and torchbearers today must take up the call to attack all forms and institutions that seek to enslave people and destroy liberty.

2. There are times in history when fighting for freedom can be dangerous. Tubman teaches us that freedom is far more valuable than personal safety and that great risk is required of those determined to preserve it.

CHAPTER 37

FROM SLAVE TO STATESMAN

66 I want to go to school." The young slave boy, covered in dust, sat petulantly down on the hearth.

His mother looked up briefly from stirring a large pot and grunted. "What in heaven's name put sich an idea in yo' head?" she asked and then continued with her labors.

"I saw Mas'r Burroughs' son in the schoolhouse, Ma. He was readin' and writin'. I want to go."

The woman shook her head. "Ain't you larned those things ain't for black folk? Why, they ketch you readin', ya be whipped, boy. Ain't legal, son. Ya be whipped good fo' sho. Ya jes' push that from yo' head; it won't do ya no good."

She began humming, and the boy knew his mother hoped he would drop the subject. But since that morning when he had passed the schoolhouse door and looked in unnoticed to watch the schoolchildren reading and writing, he couldn't stop thinking about it.

"Why cain't I learn, Ma? Why's it illegal?"

The woman set down the large spoon and shook a finger pointedly at the boy. "We ain't the same as them white folk, ya heah me?

I don't want to hear no mo' of it. Shoo!" She chased him from the kitchen, and he returned to the field.

"One day," he told himself, "I'm goin' to larn to read."

Two years later President Abraham Lincoln issued the Emancipation Proclamation, and with it that boy, his mother, and his siblings were freed from slavery.

As soon as they could secure funds, the family traveled to West Virginia to be with his stepfather, an escaped slave. With each step toward their new home the boy's excitement grew. Freedom lay ahead. That meant he could finally go to school! They arrived and settled into their new home, but neither his mother nor his stepfather said a word about school.

"Kin I go now, Ma?" he asked.

"Not yet," she replied. There were too many mouths to feed, and now that he was nine, he was old enough to go with his father to the salt furnaces each day to work.

But she noticed the longing look in his eyes every time he passed a schoolhouse, and one day when he returned home from the furnaces, he found a small book on his bed. His eyes grew wide, and he ran to his mother.

"A book! A book!" he exclaimed.

"Yes son, ya goin' to larn to read!" Every morning he arose at four in the morning so he would have time to practice his letters before heading to work. Slowly he learned to pronounce each letter; then words and then sentences took shape before his eyes. A year later, when he gained a job as a houseboy, fortune smiled on him. He was allowed to go to school for one hour a day during the winter. Finally his dreams of going to school had been realized!

The boy grew older, and as he grew, his desire to learn increased. When he heard of a university where black people were allowed to study, Hampton Institute, he determined to go there. At age sixteen, unsure where Hampton was or how he would get there, he said good-bye to his mother, stepfather, and siblings and set off on foot on a five-hundred-mile journey, with little more than the clothes on his back and the determination to earn the best education he could.

Booker T. Washington eventually arrived at Hampton High School and presented himself to the head teacher. She examined him closely and wasn't impressed. "Well," she said at last, "the recitation rooms need sweeping. See to it."

After walking five hundred miles, Booker wasn't about to let a dusty room come between him and the dream of a lifetime. He set to sweeping that room, certain that his future depended on the impression he made upon that woman. He swept the room; then he swept it again and then swept it one more time. When he was finished, he returned to the woman and announced the room was clean.

He describes the scene this way: "She was a 'Yankee' woman who knew just where to look for dirt. She took her handkerchief and rubbed it on the woodwork and about the walls. When she was unable to find one bit of dirt or dust, she quietly remarked, 'I guess you will do to enter this institution.'"

Not only did he "do," he excelled, and not long after his graduation from Hampton, he was called to help establish Tuskegee as principal of the Institute. When he assumed his position, Tuskegee had no lands or buildings. The first classes took place in a broken-down, poorly lit shanty. Washington spent his life founding and building the Institute, and by the time of his death, Tuskegee's circumstances had changed dramatically. Its annual budget was over $300,000, with an endowment of two million dollars. The one-room shanty had been replaced with more than a hundred buildings and more than two thousand acres of land. Over fifteen hundred students were instructed by almost two hundred teachers.

Washington played a significant role in helped the newly freed slaves establish and develop themselves during the tumultuous years following the Civil War. He helped organize a nationwide coalition of middle class blacks, white professionals, and church leaders. Together they worked to build economic strength and pride in black communities, with a focus on self-help, education, and entrepreneurship.

Washington was awarded a master's degree from Harvard in 1896 and later returned to speak to Harvard alumni. "We are crawling up," he told his audience, "working up, yea, burning up. Often coming up, and with proper habits, intelligence, and property, there is no power on earth that can permanently stay our progress."

From slave to salt-furnace worker, from houseboy to custodian, from Hampton to Harvard, Booker T. Washington's influence grew throughout his lifetime. His example of hard work, courage, and determination inspired a generation of men and women of all colors to remember the truth of the Founders' words, "All men are created equal," and to defend that truth in public and private.

Washington carried the torch of freedom to future generations, and in doing so, reminded us all that history is a harsh teacher and the future a demanding taskmaster. His legacy of education and cooperation should not be forgotten, and his example of courage must remain bright in the heart of every lover of liberty.

LESSONS FROM BOOKER T. WASHINGTON ON HOW TO PASS THE TORCH

1. Washington lived during a time of immense turmoil, and while many admired and applauded his efforts and actions, others criticized his methods and philosophy. Washington diplomatically helped change the status quo of his day by compromising and coordinating with those like and unlike him and, in doing so, helped secure greater liberty and prosperity for those who followed.

2. Many of freedom's torchbearers have had to fight for the education they received. Today even the poorest person has access to a self-directed education by way of libraries and the Internet with countless free educational resources. Nevertheless, the challenge of attaining an excellent education still exists, and the mandate to do so has never been greater. The need for well-educated leaders is great. Without them, nations suffer and fall. With them, the impossible becomes possible, and freedom and equality become realities that are only dreamt of during less privileged times.

PART VI

THE AGE OF WORLD WARS AND MODERN TIMES

The twentieth century is full of many lessons that relate to us today. All three forms of the Power Matrix are evident during the nineteenth and twentieth centuries: Physical Control, Land Control, and Financial Manipulation. The founding of the United States began a trend with the freedom of opportunity which has continued to spread up until current times. But freedom is a costly endeavor, requiring constant vigilance and the awareness that even war can be caused by the motive of financial gain. At the same time that the principles of freedom spread, so do the manipulators of the Power Matrix of control expand their influence.

While England and its protectorates were becoming more democratic, much of the world headed in the opposite direction. Germany was among those losing rather than gaining liberty, and its actions would come to play a crucial part in world politics

During World War I, Germany's Kaiser suspended the convertibility of its currency into gold and funded the expensive war effort through borrowing. At the close of that war, Europe demanded repayment in gold, sending Germany into rapid currency devaluation from hyperinflation. Economic chaos and instability followed, and in these precarious circumstances a figure began his rise to tyranny with the rhetoric of "restoring German nationalism."

In 1933 Adolf Hitler became chancellor of Germany. Over the next six years, using carefully crafted propaganda, he progressively pushed his country into a national frenzy. Josef Goebbels, Hitler's right-hand man, orchestrated the most thorough use of propaganda ever devised. His methods are worthy of study today, especially for those who wish to prevent something like that from recurring.

Schools were converted into training camps with state-mandated curricula, teaching a revisionist version of history. Author William Shirer wrote of this period, "Every person in the teaching profession, from kindergarten through the universities, was compelled to join the National Socialist Teachers' League." Book burning soon followed, and Shirer explained, "At about midnight a torchlight parade of thousands of students ended at a square opposite the University of Berlin. Torches were put to a huge pile of books that had been gathered there, and as the flames enveloped them more books were thrown on the fire until some twenty thousand had been consumed."

Next the media was taken over by the state. Jacques Ellul writes in his book *Propaganda*, "Hitler himself said that the bigger the lie, the more its chance of being believed. This concept leads to two attitudes among the public. The first is: 'Of course we shall not be victims of propaganda because we are capable of distinguishing truth from falsehood'.... The second attitude is: 'We believe nothing that the enemy says because everything he says is necessarily untrue.'"

We all know the results of this systematic brainwashing with its horrific consequences. The first concentration camps popped up and were converted into death camps over the next eight years. Millions of helpless Jews were incinerated and exterminated. Within six years Poland was invaded, and when the invasion was shown in newsreels, Germans cheered as they watched women and children being bayoneted.

Back in England, Prime Minister Chamberlain chose to sell a program of appeasement. He refused to acknowledge that Hitler had evil intentions and proclaimed that a peaceful solution was possible. America, even though it eventually entered the war, adopted a "hands off" policy. Far from the war's battlefront, Americans felt isolated and secure and silently watched each European country fall to the Third Reich.

There's a saying that clearly states what was happening during this period: "When good men and women stand by, evil will fill the void." Evil was indeed rising along the coasts of Europe. With the English-speaking peoples on the precipice

of extinction and Chamberlain defeated, a leadership opportunity opened up.

With all eyes on the inevitable defeat of the free world, the
British Parliament looked to someone they felt was their last
best chance, placing Sir Winston Churchill in the position of
prime minister. Churchill responded like a true historic leader.
He wrote of that time, "At last I had authority to give directions over the whole scene. I felt as if I were walking with
Destiny, and that all my past life had been but a preparation
for this hour and for this trial."

This time of world wars and Nazi and communist atrocities
has many applications to us today. All of us have doubts and
experience failure, both public and private. Sometimes we use
our doubts as an excuse not to act; often we look to failure
as a reason we cannot succeed or are not qualified for leadership opportunities. But history shows that it is during the
most insurmountable times that the unlikeliest heroes rise up.
Leaders lack only an opportunity, and when Churchill was
given that opportunity, he took it.

Each of us has opportunities today to fight oppression,
greed, intolerance, and inequity. Each of us has opportunities
to stand for liberty, equality, and justice. But will we? And
even if we will, are we prepared to do so in a way that actually
has impact?

Churchill's willingness was not all he brought to this
moment of opportunity. Just as important were his education,
his experience, and his character. Each of us must decide today
whether we will stand with torchbearers throughout history in

that uncomfortable battlefield between the enemy and victory. The enemy may be our own ignorance. The enemy may be propaganda or a platform that threatens freedom itself.

Each of us must decide whether or not we will act. And once we have decided, we must give our all to liberty's cause. For without us, she will surely fall, and who can estimate what terrible price will be required if her flame is again extinguished?

CHAPTER 38

THE NAZI NURSE WHO SAVED THE JEWS

The alleyway was dark, and in its shadowy recesses a small crowd had gathered around a short nurse. All eyes were directed downward, with backs facing outward.

The nurse's satchel was open, and her hands flew in and out of it, handing a bottle to this person, a heavy jacket to another, a small bag of grain to another. She spoke too loudly, as if aiming her words for someone who was not among the group gathered around her. "Typhoid spreads very, very rapidly. Do not expose anyone new to the illness!"

Then under her breath she responded to the hushed inquiries: "Please, Jolanta, have you any food? My baby is dying and needs nourishment!" —"Nurse, what shall I give my husband? He has a terrible fever and nausea." —"Nurse, I need a jacket! My son has nothing to keep him from freezing!"

In response to each plea she seemed to have something to ease the worries of those gathered around her. Tears of gratitude dampened each person's face as they disappeared into the evening.

Finally, the nurse turned to a young mother with a child at her knee. "You are here for your daughter?" the nurse asked expectantly, looking at the emaciated child clinging to her mother.

The mother, eyes wide with terror, nodded. She glanced furtively around before speaking. The crowd had dispersed; they remained alone in the shadowy street. Her voice was hushed. "I can't, Jolanta! I just can't!"

The nurse's face was grave. She placed a firm hand on the mother's shoulder, and responded. "You *must*, Olga. You must. Five thousand each month, that's how many are dying here in the ghetto alone; starvation, typhoid, you've seen it. And then there are those taken to Treblinka...."

The mother flinched, then pleaded, "Can you promise me, can you guarantee me she will live?" The mother glanced down at her daughter and then back to the nurse.

The nurse again looked around and then spoke. "Perhaps even I will not live to escape the ghetto today. No, I cannot promise you that." The woman's eyes shut tight as tears poured forth. The nurse grasped the mother's arm and leaned toward her to whisper, "But I can promise you, if she stays here she will die, and I promise, *promise* to return her to you, after the war." At those words the woman buried her face in her hands, stifling sobs.

"You've practiced the prayers?" the nurse asked, growing more anxious.

The mother nodded. "She knows them by heart!" she replied.

"And her Christian name?" asked the nurse. The mother again nodded. Then the nurse knelt down and spoke to mother and child. "We haven't any time to lose; we must go now!"

At those words the mother wiped her face, suddenly stoic, and pulled her daughter into a tight embrace. She spoke into her daughter's ear: "Mara, this nice woman is going to take you to a safe place, where you will have food and pretty clothes, where you will be warm and the bad men will not come, just like we talked about. You must go with her now!"

The child began to cry. "I don't want to go! I want to stay with you!" She clung tightly to her mother's knee.

"You *must* go, Mara, and I promise to come for you. Give me a hug! Now go, go! Be brave, dear Mara! Don't cry! Don't forget me!" she called out as the nurse rushed the girl toward a church.

Once inside the church, the two walked directly to a bathroom, and the nurse pulled a small dress from her satchel. *It's too small,* she said to herself, *but it must do.*

To the child she said, "Remember, your name is *Maria* now! Your mother's name is Greta, and your father's name is Boris. Tell me the names!"

The young girl timidly replied, "My name is Maria, and my mother is Greta, and Father is Boris."

"Very good. Now when you go outside, the German soldiers will be right there, and they will ask to hear the prayer. Do you remember it?" The girl nodded. "Tell it to me!" The girl recited a Catholic prayer. "Very good, very good, that will do," the nurse replied as she helped the child into the too-small dress. Her hands were shaking. She looked the girl in the eyes. "No tears; be very brave! Remember, *Maria!*"

She arose, took a deep breath, and marched from the bathroom toward a woman who waited on a bench in the back of the chapel. "Here's your daughter, *Maria*, Frau."

The woman nodded in response. "Thank you for checking her cough, I have been worried perhaps it was something serious. I am glad it is not." She grasped the child's hand. "Come, Maria! Let us go!"

The woman and girl exited the church from a different door, one that led outside the ghetto. The nurse waited anxiously at the window, holding her breath. She saw the Germans questioning the girl, and with a sigh of relief she watched Maria and the woman walk away. She collapsed onto a bench, her head in her hands.

She would never get used to this. She would never forget the sobs of the children and mothers. And she would never feel she had done enough. That woman, Irena Sendler, went home that night and added Maria's name to a long list of children whom she had taken from the ghetto. On the list was each child's Jewish birth name and his or her new "Christian" name, along with the address of each one's destination.

She placed the long list of names in a glass jar and the next day buried it under a friend's apple tree. One day, Irena promised herself, she would unearth that list for the last time and reunite those children with their parents.

Years before, in Irena's youth, her father had been one of the only physicians willing to help a nearby mostly Jewish population when a typhoid outbreak occurred. She had heard him say, "If a man is drowning, it is irrelevant what is his religion or nationality. One must help him." He had died as a result of helping those patients, but his lesson had lived on in Irena.

When the Warsaw Ghetto was instituted, an area the size of Central Park, crammed with over 450,000 Jews, Irena watched in horror. She was one of the first recruits of a group of

Jewish-sympathizers called Zegota. The group asked her to focus her efforts on rescuing Jewish children, which she willingly did.

Day in and day out, under the guise of controlling and identifying typhoid outbreaks, of which the German Nazi forces were terrified, "Jolanta" (her code name) first rescued orphaned children living on the streets of the ghetto, and then turned her efforts to smuggling out children of those still alive. Of the Warsaw Ghetto's inhabitants, 99 percent died in Treblinka, were killed in the ghetto, or died of starvation or disease there.

Due to Irena's heroic efforts, an estimated twenty-five hundred children were spared from near-certain death. She was eventually arrested and underwent severe torture. On her way to execution, the Zegota were able to bribe a Jewish officer to let Irena go instead of killing her. The next day, posters appeared throughout town announcing that she had been killed.

Irena lived in hiding until the end of the war, continuing her efforts to rescue Jewish children. The communist regime that followed the Nazi government was suspicious of her connections with Poland's resistance leaders, and she was subsequently again imprisoned and interrogated brutally. Upon her eventual release, her name was associated with anticommunist sentiments, and her heroic wartime efforts were forgotten.

Her work remained largely unknown until 1999, when a group of high school students in Kansas, in the United States, began to research her life and contributions. Amazed by her actions, they eventually produced a ten-minute play memorializing her rescue efforts, *Life in a Jar*.

Irena had nightmares her entire life of her experiences saving children in the ghetto. She was plagued by the thought that perhaps she could have done more. The early lesson of her father to save any who are drowning simply because they are drowning became her life's mantra.

Her hidden heroic efforts remind torchbearers today that life is valuable, and we each have a mandate to contribute to the safety and well-being of those around us, regardless of their similarities or differences.

LESSONS FROM IRENA SENDLER ON HOW TO PASS THE TORCH

1. Irena lived in a time when propaganda created ill-founded beliefs about the Jewish nation, which became common and widespread. The politically correct and safest route for her would have been to side with the Nazi government, and yet she chose instead, at the risk of her life, to side with the Jews in their defense. It is very easy to distance ourselves and draw distinctions between our time and past circumstances, but there are many living among us today who are refugees and victims of prejudice, violence, and hatred. We must likewise stand up for those without a voice, for in protecting their dignity and humanity, we are standing for the dignity and humanity of all people.

CHAPTER 39

THE FORGOTTEN LION

The night was pitch-black, but it was far from quiet. The steady barrage of machine-gun fire and the hail of grenades, more than six a minute, had been going on for hours.

Michael wondered if it would ever end. It was the second night of Operation Medina, a Vietnam War search-and-destroy operation, and things had turned from bad to worse. The operation had started with a helicopter assault the day before, thick in the jungles of South Vietnam. Charlie Company had been targeted early that morning by mortar and small arms fire from the People's Army of Vietnam (PAVN). The company had successfully repulsed the enemy and then continued with their operation.

The next day, however, amid deep jungle growth, the PAVN again engaged Charlie Company. The firefight resulted in the wounding of several Marines. Recognizing the danger of their position, Company C fell back and called in medevac helicopters to evacuate the wounded.

That's when the enemy acted. Using the noise of the helicopters as a cover, the PAVN moved in on two sides, undetected. While the helicopters whisked away the wounded, the enemy prepared for what they hoped would be a quick annihilation of the American forces. They outnumbered Charlie Company three or four to one and hoped to make quick work of them. Almost as soon as the helicopters were gone, the firefight resumed. As darkness fell, the fighting only intensified.

The PAVN made an aggressive attack and repeatedly tried to encircle the company. Michael, as radioman, was positioned next to the lieutenant. He was a marked target, and he knew it. The antenna of the radio he carried constantly with him was like a flag marking his every movement. What was more, the enemy knew full well that the success of the operation hinged on him. Without communication there would be no coordination, no air assistance, and no artillery support. It was easy to understand why field radio operators had a life expectancy of two weeks in the field. He'd been in Vietnam for nearly eight months now, and he knew he was testing his luck to its limits.

"Those grenades are coming from above!" Michael called out in confusion.

Lieutenant Nelson nodded and shouted back, "The enemy is in the trees!"

With the next flash of fire Michael looked up and saw in the distance a PAVN soldier, tied high in a tree, throwing down grenades. Nelson was right. He shook his head in disbelief. They were nearly surrounded, he knew that much, and were running out of ammunition quickly. The enemy was so close that the PAVN dead lay strewn among Company C's own men. The enemy's position cpuld not be seen because of the darkness, but they were very close, and their fire was not letting up.

Realizing how dire the situation was, Michael faced the near-certain prospect of death. *I've had a good life*, he reflected. *I'm ready to die, but not without a fight.* Forced into an area half the size of a football field, surrounded by three to four hundred PAVN soldiers, it was clear his time was short.

Suddenly he heard a shout. *"Let's go get some!"* Marine Jack Ruffer knew the company morale was nearly gone. In a last-ditch effort to rally the men, he began singing, or rather yelling, the Marine Hymn. "From the halls of Montezuma to the shores of Tripoli!" His comrades listened in confusion. Had he gone mad? He'd be shot any minute, drawing that much attention to himself.

Then another marine joined in. "We fight our country's battles in the air, on land and sea!" More voices began to join in, and chorus began to swell. "First to fight for right and freedom, and to keep our honor clean." Soon the jungle echoed with their rallying cry, "We are proud to claim the title of United States Marines!"

As if by magic, the men's spirits began to lift. These "Lions of Medina," as they would come to be known, renewed their desire to fight off the enemy and, if possible, live through it. That song changed the course of the battle. Though the odds were terribly against them, they fought with renewed vigor and determination to live.

Ruffer led the men in a counterattack straight into enemy lines, briefly stopping their progress. Slowly the tide began to turn. Twice more that night Company C charged directly into the pitch-dark forest path directly into enemy fire, relying only on their trust in the leader and the desire to give their all for their comrades and country. Twice more they were repulsed.

Hours later, with their ammunition all but spent, virtually everyone wounded, and few men able to stand, backup finally arrived. One marine estimated that if their backup had been delayed by even ten more minutes, they would have found all of Company C's men dead. With the arrival of fresh soldiers, they began beating back the enemy forces, and by sunrise the PAVN finally withdrew.

Many times that night Michael wondered if he would live to see the morning. He'd joined the Marines on a dare, thrilling his father and worrying his mother. In boot camp he and his fellow soldiers had been brutally torn down, and then their confidence rebuilt, ready to face whatever enemy fire would bring—or so they thought. But nothing could have prepared him for this. The faces he saw of the young men back in Camp Pendleton who had recently returned from Vietnam had warned him. Something happened there in the battlefield that was inexplicable, that was hardening and maturing and terrible. Now he understood what their faces meant.

In all, thirty-four Americans died that night. Michael was not one of them. He fought for hours until finally the enemy withdrew. After that traumatic battle Michael was sent on rest and recovery, haunted by the memories of treading so close to death's door.

Today Michael wears his Marine Corps hat and medals with pride. He limps and uses a cane. The years following the war have not been easy for him. At times life, and the memories that plague him, have seemed too much to bear. But with typical Marine determination, he has learned to call on his inner reserves again and again to meet the demons of war that visit soldiers after the battlefields are long quiet.

The Vietnam War was controversial, and when the GIs returned, there were no parades and few accolades. Popular opinion was largely against the war, and many men who fought in Vietnam said they "were never allowed to win the war." But the men and women who served there did so with conviction and purpose, firmly believing their efforts would bless and protect their families, country, and loved ones back home.

Michael is a personal friend of mine and a member of Life Leadership. He gave me the book *The Lions of Medina*, which recounts his experience in Vietnam. On the inside cover he wrote to me, "George, you are an awesome leader. The best there is, 'Semper Fi.' See you at the top." You will always find Michael limping into the Wisconsin seminars with his cane, his Marine Corps hat, and his medals. You see, he is the timekeeper who sits in the front row.

Michael's life and example serve as a fitting bookend to the biographies of men and women throughout time who have laid their lives on the line carrying the torch of freedom. Have they been forgotten? In considering their lives, callings, and courage, it's time to ask what you will do with the torch of freedom. Make no mistake—it has been handed to you.

LESSONS FROM MICHAEL ON HOW TO PASS THE TORCH

1. Study history. Learn about current events. Learn about those living today who have fought for your freedoms, and honor their efforts and memory. In an age and time when so much is on the line, we cannot afford to be complacent or ignorant.

2. Every person has something unique to contribute to the cause of liberty. What will you offer in service to the torch of freedom? If you don't know, don't rest until you've learned why it is you're here and what it is you were sent to give. Then spend the rest of your days pursuing that purpose and giving that gift. The world will be better for it.

WHAT WILL WE DO WITH THE TORCH OF FREEDOM?

Great leaders from the past have kept the torch of freedom aflame and have handed it to us.

We are at a critical time in history. Few people have studied the lessons from the past. The torch of freedom is barely flickering—and may soon be completely extinguished without bold and selfless action from leaders willing to do the work necessary to keep the flame burning bright. Increasing our literacy with self-directed education is one of the most important things we can do. As has been said many times, not all readers are leaders, but all leaders are readers.

We are witnessing an overall decline in global leadership. Literacy in our country is at an all-time low. Studies show that at the turn of the 1900s literacy in America was as high as 90 percent. It has gradually decreased since the 1940s, when it was in the 70 percent range. Today, depending on which studies you consult, as many as three out of four Americans read not a single book in the course of a year. That decline in literacy should shock us.

The ramifications for people who are not reading and not thinking are widespread. Christopher Lasch writes about the effects of the growing trend in illiteracy in *The Culture of Narcissism*, pointing out that "it has contributed to the decline of critical thought and the erosion of intellectual standards." Ultimately, if we don't think, someone else will think for us. This is evidence of why we are seeing a growing trend toward central state control. And as Frederic Bastiat tried to warn us, "So long as taxes were collected by force to subsidize a public educational system, no genuine freedom of choice could be present for the parent in the education of his own children."

Urukagina changed the world with the spread of the written word. The Greeks and Romans expanded on literacy with the invention of "leisure." The printing press brought about prosperous conditions throughout civilization as never before. Slaves broke from their bondage with increased literacy. Hitler tried to oppress freedom by burning the books, but the torch of freedom was passed on.

Noah Webster, in the 1800s, said about his time, "The minds of the youth are perpetually led to the history of Greece and Rome where boys and girls are constantly repeating the declamations of Demosthenes and Cicero." They learned that the word *idiot* comes from the Greek word *idiotes*, meaning one who puts private pleasures before public affairs and hence is ignorant of what really matters in life.

Roman historian Livy wrote something that hits too close to home as the Roman Empire fell: "Trace the progress of our moral decline, to watch first the sinking of the foundations of morality as the old ways were allowed to lapse, then the rapidly increasing disintegration, the final collapse of the whole edifice. Then the dark dawning of the modern day when we can neither endure our vices nor face the remedies needed to cure them."

Historian Thomas Carlyle wrote, "The Great Man was always as lightning out of Heaven: the rest of men waited for him as fuel and then they too would flame." The flame has been passed on through the torch of freedom from these underground historical leaders. What will we do with it?

At times it can seem like the odds against reviving the torch of freedom are insurmountable. The tide of popular opinion rises strongly against us.

When we feel that opposition, we must think of people like Michael and Sendler, Barnabas and Wycliffe, Rutherford and Locke. Think of Greene and Kitto and Booker T. Washington. We are in the company of angels, soldiers, and statesmen. We must draw on their strength and remember that without their efforts coupled with our own, liberty's life expectancy is short.

Study them. Remember them. Join with them in defending the torch of freedom so we may continue to be free to live up to our God-given potential. Regardless of the cost, will you help to pass the torch of freedom?

God Bless,
George Guzzardo

ACKNOWLEDGEMENTS

Thanks goes to Jill Guzzardo. You are a blessing to have by my side. You've been amazingly patient while helping me with the initial editing of this book. I love you.

Thank you, Orrin and Laurie Woodward. You've been great friends, mentors, and business partners for twenty-plus years now. Not many people can say that they have been blessed with that type of relationship. I love you guys.

Thanks to the LIFE Leadership business. You've given me the personal, professional, and financial information to allow me to have a self-directed education and ultimately a platform to write this book.

My ultimate thanks go to my Lord and Savior Jesus Christ, whose grace and mercy came into my life. You make all things possible. My prayer is that Your Holy Spirit works through this book and that it glorifies You and Your world.

FOR FURTHER READING

Adair, John. *Inspiring Leadership*.

Allmand, Christopher. *The Hundred Years War*.

Beale, David. *The Mayflower Pilgrims*.

Berkin, Carrol. *Revolutionary Mothers*.

Bishop, Morris. *The Middle Ages*.

Burns, James. *Revivals: Their Laws and Their Leaders*.

Cartlege, Paul. *The Spartans*.

Christian History Magazine. *131 Christians Everyone Should Know*.

Commager, Henry Steele. *Churchill's History of the English Speaking People*.

Cowan, Louise, and Os Guinness. *Invitation to the Classics*.

Creasy, Edward S. *15 Decisive Battles of the World*.

Deane, Anthony. *Undiscovered Ocean*.

DeMille, Oliver, and Orrin Woodward. *Leadershift*.

Duckett, Eleanor Shipley. *Alfred the Great: The King and His England*.

Ellul, Jacques. *Propaganda*.

Fedele, Gene. *Heroes of the Faith*.

Fisher, Antony. *Must History Repeat Itself?*.

Gamble, Richard M. *The Great Tradition*.

Glass, Doyle E. *The Lions of Medina*.

Grant, Callie Smith. *Harriet Tubman*.

Gregg II, Gary L. *Vital Remnants*.

Hedges, Chris. *Empire of Illusion*.

Hedrick, Larry. *Xenophon's Cyrus the Great*.

Herman, William. *Hearts Courageous*.

Houghton, S. M. *Sketches From Church History*.

Kagan, Donald. *Pericles of Athens*.

Kirk, Russell. *The Roots of American Order*.

Langguth, A. J. *Patriots*.

Lasch, Christopher. *Culture of Narcissism*.

Lyman, Richard W., and Louis W. Spitz. *Major Crises in Western Civilization*.

Mansfield, Stephen. *Forgotten Founding Father*.

Michael, Larry J. *Spurgeon on Leadership*.

Powell, Jim. *The Triumph of Liberty*.

Richard, Carl J. *Twelve Greeks and Romans Who Changed the World*.

Richard, Carl J. *The Greeks and Romans Bearing Gifts*.

Roberts, Cokie. *Founding Mothers*.

Roche, George. *Free Markets, Free Men*.

Rose, Matthew F. *John Witherspoon*.

Shearer, Robert G. *Famous Men of the Renaissance and Reformation*.

Shirer, William. *The Rise and Fall of the Third Reich*.

Spitz, Lewis W. *The Renaissance and the Reformation Movements*.

Stewart, Chris, and Ted Stewart. *7 Tipping Points That Saved the World*.

Vaughan, David J. *A Divine Light*.

Vaughn, David J. *The Pillars of Leadership*.

Woodward, Orrin. *The Financial Matrix*.

Woodward, Orrin. *And Justice for All*.

NOTES

1   Fornara-Samons, *Athens from Cleisthenes to Pericles*, 24–25
2   K. Paparrigopoulos, Aa, 241–42
3   Cicero, De Oratore, 3.213 (G. Kennedy, "Oratory", 517-18)
4   Demosthenes, *Third Phillipic*, 65; (D.M. MacDoweel, Demosthenes the Orator, ch. 13)
5   Demosthenes Second Olynthiac, 10
6   Plutarch, Demosthenes, 13.1
7   Longinus, *On the Sublime*, 12.4, 34.4 (D.C. Innes, "Longinus and Caecilius", 277-279)
8   Francis Petrarch, Letter to Cicero
9   Zielínski, Taeusz. *Cicero Im Wandel Der Jahrhunderte*. Nabu Press
10 Murray Rothbard, *Economic Thought Before Adam Smith*, Section 1.9
11 Cicero, *Selected Works*, 1971, 24
12 Orrin Woodward, "The Financial Matrix and Rome's Collapse"
13 Tacitus, *Agricola*, ch. 44-45, Oxford Revised Translation
14 Ibid.
15 Acts 4:36
16 Acts 15:39
17 Colossians 4:10–11

18   Eusibius, The Ecclesiastical History, Book Five, 2.1-2

19   *The Wanderer*, old Anglo Saxon poem circa 700-1000 AD.

20   Churchill, Winston. *A History of the English-Speaking Peoples, Vol 1:Birth of Britain.*

21   Brown, Patricia F. (1997) Venice & Antiquity: The Venetian Sense of the Past. Yale University Press. 49

22   Louis W. Spitz, Professor of History at Stanford, Manuscript

23   Council of Constance 1414–1418, papalencyclicals.net

24   Schaff, Philipp & David S Schaff, *History of the Christian Church*, vol. 5 part 2, 325

25   Townsend, George (1844) *The Acts and Monuments of John Foxe*, vol. 3, 96

26   *Selections from the Hengwrt Mss. Preserved in the Peniarth Library*. Williams, Robert, ed. & trans. London: Thomas Richards, 1892

27   Savonarola, Letter I: To his father, Nicolas Savonarola, Bologna, 25 April 1475, excerpts

28   *"Humanism". The Cambridge Dictionary of Philosophy, Second Edition*. Cambridge University Press. 1999. 397

29   DeMille, Oliver (2010). *Why Societies Decline, Part I: The Positive Effects of Adversity*. TheSocialLeader.com retrieved from: http://www.thesocialleader.com/2010/10/societies-decline-positive-effects-adversity/ April 21, 2016.

30   Speech to the First Protectorate Parliament, 4 September 1654, (Roots 1989, 42)

31   Josiah Quincy, "Memoir of the Life of John Quincy Adams." 79-80

32   The Autobiography of Benjamin Franklin (Houghton, Mifflin and Company, 1888), 131

33 Mansfield, Stephen. *Forgotten Founding Father: The Heroic Legacy of George Whitfield.*

34 Hoffer, Peter C., (2011) When Benjamin Franklin Met the Reverend Whitefield: Enlightenment, Revival, and the Power of the Printed Word (Witness to History)

35 Adams, John

36 Congressional Record, Volume 147-Part 14. Oct 11, 2001-Oct 24, 2001; 20222

37 Montesquieu, "The Spirit of the Laws." Book 11, chapter 6, "Of the Constitution of England."

38 Weaver, Richard M. (1948). "Ideas Have Consequences."

39 Judith Sargent Murray to her parents, August 14, 1790   in From Gloucester to Philadelphia in 1790: Observations, Anecdotes, and Thoughts from the Eighteenth-Century Letters of Judith Sargent Murray (Cambridge, Mass.: Judith Sargent Murray Society, 1998), 54

40 http://marthawashington.us/exhibits/show/ martha-washington--a-life/life-at-mt--vernon-before-the-/ page-3

41 Rousseau, "Social Contract," Real Property

42 Conversation based on text from Bastiat's work, "Property and Law" from Essays on Political Economy

43 Lost Senses — Deafness.' By John Kitto, D.D., 11-12

44 Pollock, John (1977), Wilberforce, New York: St. Martin's Press, 58

45 Bradford, Sarah Hopkins (1971) (orig. pub. 1869), Scenes in the Life of Harriet Tubman. Freeport: Books for Libraries Press. 19

George Guzzardo

After completing his college degree in Chicago, George moved to Michigan's Upper Peninsula with his wife Jill. Over the next twenty years, George worked in a private Physical Therapy practice where he pioneered a state of the art industrial wellness program for the mining and forest industry. In addition, George was active in sports medicine and stress management.

George's passion to help people was rekindled after partnering with bestselling author and leadership expert Orrin Woodward. They became job optional after learning about the leadership and financial principles taught in Life Leadership. This new found autonomy led to the opportunity to relocate into the foothills of Tucson, Arizona where he now resides full-time. He and Jill own a private eight acre retreat where they enjoy rescue horses, nature trails, photography, and off-road four-wheel driving in the mountains behind their Tucson home. It has been particularly fulfilling to be able to assist a local non-profit organization involved in helping children and their families. George and Jill enjoy spending time with their grandchild and helping friends succeed in the Life Leadership business.

George currently mentors aspiring leaders across the world. He speaks to thousands about leadership and leads communities all across the country. Read George's blog at: georgeguzzardo.typepad.com.

Books in the Life Leadership Essentials Series

***Mentoring Matters: Targets, Techniques, and Tools for Becoming a Great Mentor* with Foreword by Orrin Woodward**
Get your sticky notes ready for all the info you're about to take in from this book. Do you know what it means to be a *great* mentor? It's a key part of successful leadership, but for most people, the necessary skills and techniques don't come naturally. Educate yourself on all of the key targets, techniques, and tools for becoming a magnificent mentor with this easy-to-apply manual. Your leadership success will be forever increased!

***Turn the Page: How to Read Like a Top Leader* with Introduction by Chris Brady**
Leaders are readers. But there are many ways to read, and leaders read differently than most people do. They read to learn what they need to know, do, or feel, regardless of the author's intent or words. They see past the words and read with the specific intent of finding truth and applying it directly in their own lives. Learn how to read like a top leader so you'll be better able to emulate their success. Applying the skills taught in *Turn the Page* will impact your life, career, and leadership abilities in ways you can't even imagine. So turn the page and start reading!

***SPLASH!: A Leader's Guide to Effective Public Speaking* with Foreword by Chris Brady**
For many, the fear of giving a speech is worse than the fear of death. But public speaking can be truly enjoyable *and* a powerful tool for making a difference in the lives of others. Whether you are a beginner or a seasoned orator, this book will help you transform your public speaking to a whole new level of leadership influence. Learn the SPLASH formula for great public speaking that will make you the kind of speaker and leader who makes a SPLASH—leaving any audience, big or small, forever changed—every time you speak!

The Serious Power of Fun with Foreword by Chris Brady

Life got you down? Feeling like life isn't much fun is a bad place to be. Fun matters. It is serious business and a source of significant leadership power. Without it, few people maintain the levels of inspired motivation and sustained effort that bring great success. So put a smile back on your face. Discover how to make every area of life more enjoyable and turn any situation into the right kind of fun. Learn to cultivate a habit of designed gratification—where life just keeps getting better—and *laugh your way to increased success* with *The Serious Power of Fun!*

Wavemakers: How Small Acts of Courage Can Change the World with Foreword by Chris Brady

Every now and then, extraordinary individuals come along who make huge waves and bring about permanent change in the lives of so many that society as a whole is forever altered. Discover from the examples of the various "Wavemakers" showcased in this book how you can make waves of your own and change the world for the better!

Dealing with Difficult People with Foreword by Chris Brady

How many times have you felt like banging your head against the wall trying to figure out how to deal with a routinely difficult person, whether at work or in your personal life? You can't control others, but you can control how you handle them. Learn about the seven main types of difficult people and the Five-Step Peace Process, and equip yourself to understand why people behave the way they do, break the cycle of frustration, and turn your interactions into healthy, productive experiences. "You are going to encounter difficult people. Plan on it. Prepare for it. Become good at it."

Financial Fitness for Teens: 6 Steps from Broke to Abundant with Foreword **by Chris Brady**

It's never too early to learn the principles of financial success. But schools often skip right over this crucial topic. And by the time many adults figure out that they don't know how to properly manage their money, they are often buried in debt and feeling helpless to dig themselves out. *Financial Fitness for Teens* aims to fill in the gap, break the cycle of bad financial habits and misinformation being passed down from generation to generation, and show youth how easy and exciting financial fitness can be. "The money thing" is one of the most important aspects of life to master—and the sooner, the better!

Conflict Resolution: The 8 Vital Principles with **Foreword by Bill Lewis**

Conflict Resolution is more than just reading words in a book. It's about utilizing what you learn in order to keep moving forward without negative baggage and drama. Tend to difficult situations properly, and instead of winning battles, you will win allies. This book will completely equip you to learn how to handle situations with grace, calmness, and strength. It takes courage to resolve conflict rather than to just run from it or ignore it. Your quality of life depends on it. With the right information, properly applied, your life can be peacefully productive.

Ladder: Climbing Out of a Slump with **Foreword by Dan Hawkins**

Stuck in a rut and feeling your dreams are out of reach? Stop listening to the negative voices telling you success is too hard and that you aren't good enough. Your slump is screaming that it's time for a change. And the Slump-to-Success Ladder is your friend that will help you turn your slump into increased success. Once you know the art of climbing the simple but powerful Six Rungs of the Slump-to-Success Ladder, you will have much more control over where you end up. So when a slump comes, you will smile and enthusiastically start climbing the Ladder right away, knowing that success is on the way!

Revolutionary leadership **with Foreword by Orrin Woodward**
Leadership is important to everyone in every endeavor in life. We are all called upon to lead at some point, and usually several points, in our lives. But leadership is a lot like art - difficult to define but we know it when we see it. For that reason this book presents the concept of leadership through the achievements of several great individuals, none of whom were perfect, but all of whom grasped the leadership challenge of their time and performed remarkably. Become the best leader you can be by learning from their examples!

Thick-Skinned **with Foreword by Claude Hamilton**
The downfall of many people is in worrying what others think, sometimes to the detrimental point of losing their motivation and giving up. Thick skin is the exact ingredient that can help those who are looking to round out this area of their lives that often holds them back. This book will help you figure out why you are thin-skinned, show you how to ignore the negative speak from others and focus on positive thoughts instead, and teach you ways to develop thicker skin so you can flourish without hesitation.

Paradigm Shift **with Foreword by George Guzzardo**
A paradigm shift is a sudden, major change in the way you view something, brought on by new information or a new detail that was formerly unknown. Paradigm shifts occur in every area of life, dramatically impacting everyone they touch and leaving a legacy of large-scale transformation in their path. This book is about seven such paradigm shifts, seven major emerging changes, that will rock the world in the years and decades just ahead.

Innovator with Foreword by Bill Lewis

No matter how successful you've been up to this point, if you want continued success or greater success in your life, it's time to innovate now—because it's always time to innovate. Behind every success and all advancement stands the Innovator. Unfortunately, successful and consistent innovation is elusive for most people. So how exactly do we innovate? And how do we restore ourselves to a society of innovators? We need to learn from those who have successfully taken on the role of the Innovator, the brave souls who dare to think that the system can be improved and who set out to improve it against all odds. The few who figure out how to effectively innovate and continually apply the process naturally achieve top leadership in their chosen field.

Point and Grunt with Foreword by Claude Hamilton

Communication is a broad topic, one which includes public speaking, small group meetings, interpersonal conversation, crucial conversations, negotiations, e-mails, texting, social media, and more. In fact, when it comes down to it, communication is an enormous part of our lives. Yet how much training do any of us receive in these various areas? When and where do we learn timeless principles and timely techniques? How do we determine our effectiveness and how to improve? Most of us, if we're honest, would have to admit that our ability to communicate is not something that usually receives our direct attention at all, much less an effort to intentionally improve it. But that all ends with this groundbreaking book! Easy to read but important to understand, the concepts inside will refresh the skills you already have and inform you in areas you may not have considered.

Mindset memos with Foreword by Chris Brady

When confronted with the success of others, in any field, one is quickly able to gather details of their achievements, such as the steps, the people, and the circumstances of what they did. What is harder to determine, however, is how they knew to do what they did. Often when looking from the outside at the success of another, it is easy to conclude that the path to fame and fortune for them was clear-cut and obvious. But when attempting to look through their eyes instead, one sees a much more compelling perspective. Learning how they knew to do what they did that made them successful is what this book is all about. In short, bite-sized biographies, the true stories of success in these pages are designed to give you insight into knowing what to do in your own life in order to bring about the success and significance you desire.